Can Mother Goose Come Down to Play?

Diane White

Humanics Learning
Atlanta, Georgia

Humanics Learning
P.O. Box 7447
Atlanta, Georgia 30309

First Printing 1990

© Copyright 1990 Humanics Limited

PRINTED IN THE UNITED STATES OF AMERICA

Library of Congress Cataloging-in-Publication Data

White, Diane, 1955-
  Can Mother Goose come down to play?

  1. Education, Preschool--Activity programs.
2. Nursery rhymes--Study and teaching (Preschool)
I. Title.
LB1140.35.C74W47 1989   372.13'32   89-26679
ISBN 0-89334-136-3

Illustrations by Jeff Sasser and Elaine Commins.

Table of Contents

INTRODUCTION

Can Mother Goose come down to play? Of course she can, and with all of her sometimes peculiar friends, too. For generations, Mother Goose has earned her place on children's bookshelves throughout the world. Her rhythm and rhymes have blended wonderfully with the swaying rocking chairs that lull children to sleep. Now it's time to take Mother Goose down from the shelf, dust her off a bit, and bring her right into the middle of the day's activities.

All adults working with children, whether they are parents, day care providers, or teachers, search for fun new ways to spend special time with their children. The activities in this book utilize favorite nursery rhymes as springboards into all of the curriculum areas to which young people should be exposed. At first glance, everything might appear to be just fun and games, but I like to keep in my mind that play is a child's best learning tool. Through these activities, Mother Goose can help teach math, problem-solving skills, language development, science, music, and dramatic involvement, as well as many other skills. The concepts and skills that each activity stresses are listed at its conclusion. Sometimes, artistic inhibitions get in the way of some great times with children, so full-size patterns are provided for everything that might require a flair.

I hope you enjoy the little people in your life, and indulge them in the nonsensical wonders of Mother Goose. Share in making Little Jack Horner's Thumb Plums, writing an original version of Mary Had A Little Lamb, and growing Little Boy Blue's Shoe Meadows and Cornfields. Together, experience the occupations of the Butcher, the Baker, and the Candlestick Maker. Design an unbreakable Humpty Dumpty, and wash the Three Little Kittens' soiled mittens. Let Mother goose come down to play! Do it for your children - and for the fun of it!

Diane White

LITTLE MISS MUFFET

Little Miss Muffet
Sat on a tuffet
Eating her curds and whey
Along came a spider
Who sat down beside her
And frightened Miss Muffet away!

GROUPTIME ACTIVITIES

1. Sing "Little Miss Muffet" to the tune of "This Is the Way We Wash Our Clothes":

    Little Miss Muffet sat on her tuffet,
    Sat on her tuffet, sat on her tuffet,
    Little Miss Muffet sat on her tuffet,
    Eating her curds and whey.

    Along came a spider who sat down beside her,
    Sat down beside her, sat down beside her,
    Along came a spider who sat down beside her,
    And frightened Miss Muffet away!

2. Have the children dramatize the rhyme while saying it together. Encourage them to stoop down and sit on a tuffet (see Activity 9 in this section), and pretend to eat curds and whey. Tell them to let their hands be creeping spiders that sit down beside them and have them jump up and yell "Eek!" Repeat the actions, this time without using words.

3. Put up a black flannel spider body *(See Pattern 1)* without any legs on the flannelboard. Count with the children as eight flannel spider legs are put on the body. Try counting backwards as the legs are taken off again.

4. Let the children pretend that their hands are spiders. Direct the spiders to go *on, over, under, behind, beside, beneath, above, in front of*, and *in back of* the children. Make all of the spiders disappear by having the children stretch their hands and fingers into the air. *POOF!*

5. Share close-up pictures of spiders and webs from library books and magazines. Encourage the children to describe the pictures. Discuss some hypothetical situations like: Would a spider rather live in a house or outside? How might a spider feel when a big person came near him? If a spider was seen inside of a house, what could be done about it? How could a spider be made happy?

Pattern 1

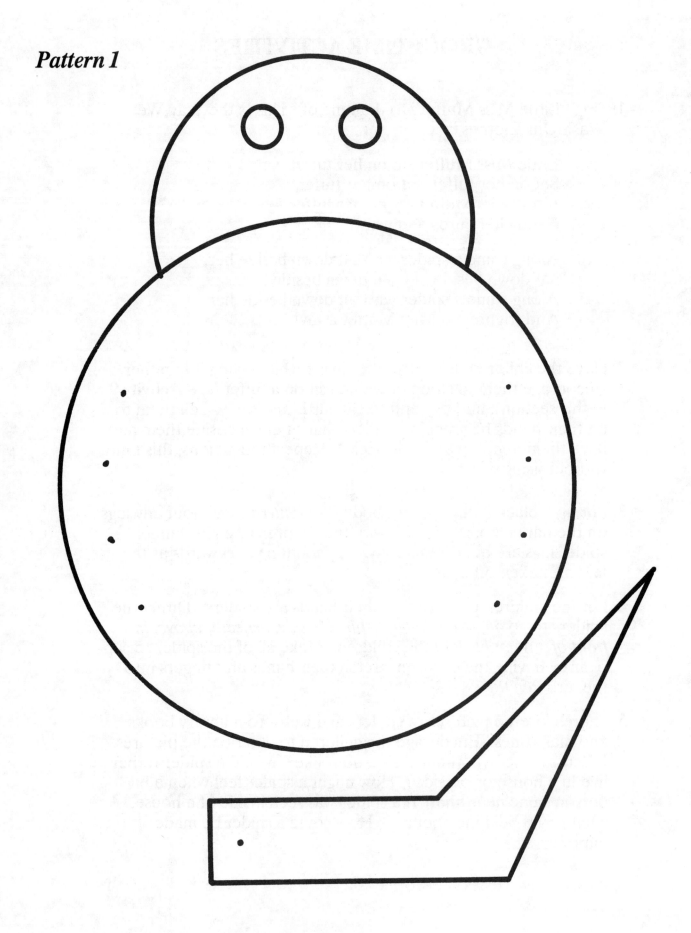

6. Read *The Very Busy Spider,* by Eric Carle (Philomel Books, 1984). This book depicts the creation of a spider web using relief illustrations for the children to feel.

Grouptime Concepts: spatial awareness, disappearance, spiders, webs are spiders' homes.

Grouptime Skills: singing, dramatic involvement, counting, observation, describing, problem solving, hypothesizing.

SMALL GROUP ACTIVITIES

1. GROSS MOTOR
Spider Webs

- Give the children partial rolls of toilet paper. Encourage them to pretend to be spiders spinning webs.
- Let them "spider web" the room with the paper, crawling over chairs and under tables.
- Make the webs all disappear by having the children roll the paper up again.

Concepts: a spider web is a crisscross pattern, every web is unique.

Skills: climbing, crawling, rolling, unrolling, dramatic involvement.

2. FINE MOTOR:
Moveable Spiders

- Cut out a black construction paper spider body and eight spider legs *(See Pattern 1)* for each child. Punch eight holes on each spider body where the legs should go. Punch a hole in one end of each leg.
- Let the children put brass fasteners through the holes to attach the moveable legs to the spider bodies. Add peel-and-stick hole reinforcers or two more brass fasteners for eyes.
- For more fun, attach a piece of yarn to the spider so it can be hung from the ceiling or dangled from the children's wrists.

Concepts: a spider has eight legs and two eyes, it's legs are moveable.

Skills: manipulation of paper and brass fasteners, one-to-one correspondence.

3. EYE/HAND COORDINATION
Spider Web Lacing Plates

- Cut the middle, flat circle out of a paper plate and discard it.

- Punch varied holes around the remaining paper plate ring.

- Attach a long piece of yarn to the plate for the child to lace through the holes and across the open middle of the ring.

- Stiffen the end of the yarn by dipping it in hot wax or by wrapping masking tape around it. This will make "lacing" with the yarn much easier. *(Illustration 1)* Have the children thread the yarn through the holes and back and forth across the plate to create a spider web of their own.

Concepts: one can see through spider webs, each web is different.

Skills: lacing, creativity.

4. NUTRITION
Miss Muffet's Curds and Whey

    1 cup milk
    1 1/2 tsp. vinegar
    salt, garlic salt, or onion salt

- Pour milk into a small saucepan. Stir milk constantly over medium heat until bubbles appear.

- Remove from heat and stir in vinegar. Curds will form almost immediately.

- Pour mixture through a tea strainer, cheesecloth, or clean nylon to separate curds and whey.

- Press the curds gently to remove any excess whey.

- Season the curds as desired and serve on crackers or rice cakes.

Concepts: boiling, straining, curds and whey.

Skills: stirring, squeezing, straining, spreading.

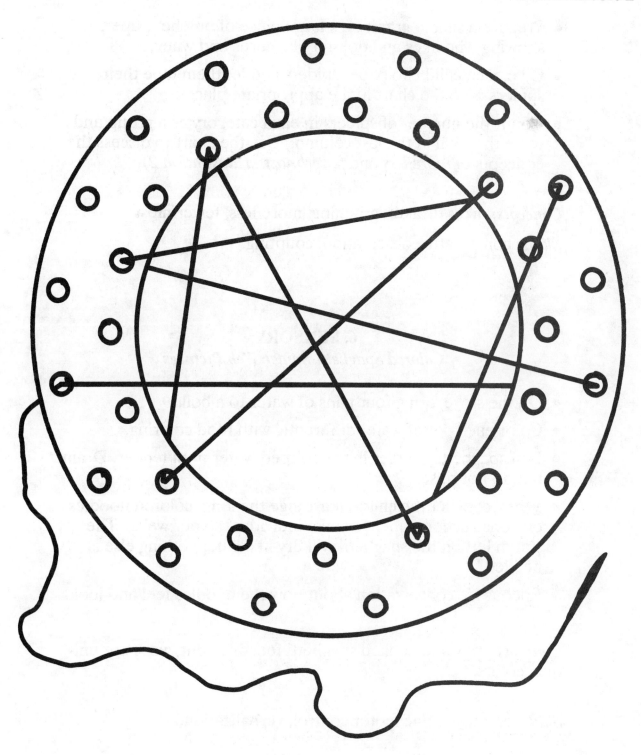

5. MATH
A Curds and Whey Graph

- Prepare a simple graph on a large piece of butcher paper, showing who likes and doesn't like curds and whey.

- Give each child two paper spiders and let them tape their spiders onto the chart in the appropriate places.

- Count the number of spiders in each category as a group and write the total in the last column. Use the chart to discuss the concepts of *more/less* and *fewer/most*. *(Illustration 2)*

Concepts: likes/dislikes, graphing, more/less, fewer/most.

Skills: comparative observation, counting.

6. SENSORY
Colored Spaghetti Spider Web Pictures

- On the stove, bring four pans of water to a boil.

- Color each pot of water differently with food coloring.

- Boil spaghetti noodles in the colored water until tender. Drain, but do not rinse.

- When cool, let the children arrange the long, colored noodles on construction paper to make individual spider webs. The starch left on the spaghetti will dry like glue; nothing else is needed.

- Encourage conversation about how the noodles feel and look.

Concepts: raw and cooked spaghetti feel different, webs are unique, colors.

Skills: creativity, fine motor control, verbalization.

2		I Like Curds on Crackers.
4		I Don't Like Curds on Crackers
0		I Like Whey.
3		I Don't Like Whey

7. SCIENCE
Real Spiders!

- Real spiders are fascinating to observe. If possible, let the children help collect some live specimens. Jars with perforated lids, or screen cylinders with foil pie-pan tops and bottoms, make great temporary homes for spiders.

- Give the spiders sticks and stones to crawl on and hide behind, to make observation more interesting.

- Offer the children magnifying glasses to use and have spider picture books from the library nearby for comparison.

- Verbalization can be encouraged by talking about how spiders catch their food, where spiders live, and captivity versus freedom.

- After a day of observation, have the children decide on a suitable spot outside and let the spiders go.

- Explain that the released spiders will now make new webs to capture the food that they need. *(Illustration 3)*

Concepts: what spiders look like, how they move, where they live, what they do.

Skills: observation, comparing, verbalization, decision making.

8. ART
Magic Spider Webs

- Let the children use cotton swabs to paint liquid bleach onto black construction paper. Their spider web designs will slowly appear in a faded orange-like color.

- Different colors of paper produce different color designs.

- This activity needs to be supervised *very* closely in a small group setting, but it's worth the extra effort.

Concepts: surprise, cause, and effect.

Skills: painting, creativity.

Illustration 3

9. BLOCKS
Building Tuffets and Spider Webs

- Explain that tuffets are low seats or stools.

- Challenge the children to use blocks to make a tuffet to sit on, and encourage the dramatization of the "Little Miss Muffet" rhyme.

- Offer a second challenge, this time to use the blocks to make one big flat web together.

- The children can then pretend they are giant spiders walking on the huge block spider web they have just created.

Concepts: tuffets and spider webs.

Skills: flat and upright block building, individual and cooperative building, dramatic play.

WEE WILLIE WINKIE

Wee Willie Winkie,
Runs through the town,
Upstairs and downstairs,
In his nightgown;
Rapping at the window,
Crying through the lock,
"Are the children in their beds?
For now it's eight o'clock."

GROUPTIME ACTIVITIES

1. Sing "Wee Willie Winkie" to the tune of "The ABC Song", repeating the first four lines at the conclusion of the song.

2. Discuss the children's individual bedtime rituals. Do they first take a bath, brush their teeth, and then go to bed? Do they always read a story before bed, or have a glass of milk? Do they have a special time they go to bed each night? Have a "bedtime bag" full of common bedtime-ritual items to share with the children. Items to include might be: a hairbrush, toothbrush and toothpaste, washcloth, book, empty milk carton and cup, teddy bear, blanket, pajamas, robe, and slippers.

3. Actions are fun to incorporate while repeating nursery rhymes. Try using these:

   > Wee Willie Winkie, *(point to self)*
   > Runs through the town, *(stomp feet)*
   > Upstairs and downstairs, *(stand up, sit down)*
   > In his nightgown; *(arms around self - cold!)*
   > Rapping at the window, *(pretend to knock)*
   > Crying through the lock, *(cup hands around mouth)*
   > "Are the children in their beds? *(pretend to sleep)*
   > For now its eight o'clock. *"(show eight fingers)*

4. Engage the children in some silly rhyming fun. Instead of Wee Willie Winkie doing all of the antics, try substituting a few of the following while the children repeat the rhyme:

   > Bee Billy Binkie, *buzzing through the town, ...*
   > Gee Golly Grimpie, *galumphing ...*
   > He's Hilly Hinkie, *hopping ...*
   > Me Mighty Minkie, *motors ...*
   > See Silly Sinkie, *strutting ...*
   > Tea Totalling Twinkie, *tiptoes ...*

   - See if the children are able to recognize the repeating beginning consonant in each phrase. This is called "alliteration."

Grouptime Concepts: bedtime rituals, rhyming, humor.

Grouptime Skills: singing new words to a familiar tune, learning a new fingerplay.

SMALL GROUP ACTIVITIES

1. DRAMATIC PLAY
Pajama Party Time!

- Invite the children to a daytime pajama party.

- Let them wear pajamas, robes ,and slippers, converse with favorite stuffed animals, and make pretend beds out of blankets on the floor.

- Alarm clocks can provide a lot of fun, as can music from some of the children's favorite records and tapes.

- Perhaps pop some popcorn for a treat and enjoy some cozy storytimes in a rocking chair.

- This activity is fun to do before naptime, so that "Wee Willie Winkie" can really announce that it's time for all children to be in their beds.

    Concepts: bedtime rituals.

    Skills: dramatic involvement.

2. SCIENCE
Flashlight Dancing

- Flashlights are great fun to use in the dark, and Willie probably would have loved having one instead of his lantern!

- Turn out the lights and spotlight the children with one or more flashlights, as they dance to music.

- For an old-time movie effect, wiggle the flashlights back and forth quickly on the moving children.

- Point the individual children's shadows on the nearby walls.

- Let the children experiment with shadow imagery.

Concepts: dark, light, shadows, flickering motions can be simulated by moving lights.

Skills: experimentation.

3. EYE/HAND COORDINATION
Keys and Locks

- Keys seem to be a time-tested love of all children. Give the children a collection of padlocks and keys and let them enjoy locking and unlocking to their hearts' content.

- The trial and error approach to matching keys with locks may be frustrating to some children, so they might appreciate having the keys and locks color-coded.

Concepts: locked versus unlocked, keys can unlock locks, trial and error matching.

Skills: eye/hand coordination, color matching (if keys and locks are color coded).

4. BLOCKS
Windows, Beds, Stairs, and Stars

- "Wee Willie Winkie" can provide wonderful springboards for block building creativity. Hang some paper stars and a moon from the ceiling over the block area and repeat the nursery rhyme with the children.

- Is there anything from Willie's world that could be built out of blocks? How about building some stairs for him to run up and down? Or, give the children some dolls to build beds for, along with some blankets and doll pajamas.

- Trying to construct buildings with windows to "rap" at would also be a good challenge for experienced block builders.

Concepts: objects from an imaginary world can be built out of blocks.

Skills: dramatic involvement, transforming ideas into block structures.

5. ART
Window Prints

- Children love to look out the window, especially when falling asleep. Let them each paint a picture of what they see out their window, on a piece of hard, flat plastic that's about 8" x 10".

- When a painting is complete, turn the plastic over and press it paint side down, onto a fresh piece of construction paper.

- Rinse the plastic off and dry it for other children to use.

- When the prints are dry, mount them behind larger pieces of construction paper that have been cut like window frames. *(Illustration 4)*

Concepts: printmaking.

Skills: creativity, painting, imagination.

Illustration 4

6. GROSS MOTOR
Eight O'clock, Bedtime !

- This game is similar to "Red Light, Green Light". The children line up at the starting line, with one person as Wee Willie Winkie standing at the finish line.

- Willie determines how the children should move, whether it be by hopping, crawling, or skipping.

- When Willie calls out different times of the day such as two o'clock, or seven o'clock, the children are free to move toward Willie.

- When Willie calls out, "Eight o'clock, bedtime!" the children must immediately drop to a sleeping position on the ground.

- Children who continue to move must go back to the starting line.

- Play is continued until someone reaches Willie at the finish line. That child then becomes Willie, and the game is started over again.

Concepts : games have rules, and following rules makes game playing more fun.

Skills: gross motor skills used in locomotion, listening, cooperation.

LITTLE BOY BLUE

Little Boy Blue
Come blow your horn.
The sheep's in the meadow,
The cow's in the corn.

Where is the boy
Who looks after the sheep?
He's under the haystack
Fast asleep.

Will you wake him?
No, not I!
For if I do,
He's sure to cry.

GROUPTIME ACTIVITIES

1. Introduce "Little Boy Blue" by displaying an illustration of the rhyme. Ask the children what they see and what might be happening in the picture.

2. Use "Little Boy Blue" flannel pieces *(See Pattern 3)* on a flannelboard, while saying the rhyme. Repeat it, encouraging the children to chime in. By displaying the flannel pieces at the appropriate times, even the children who don't know the rhyme will be able to fill in the key words.

3. Rhythmically chant the rhyme, using dramatic actions when appropriate. Try whispering the last verse.

4. Tape record the children making the following sounds in this order: *horn blowing, baa, moo, baa, snoring,* and *crying.* Play each sound to the group, asking them who or what made the sound, and where the sound was made. For example, the sheep said "baa" in the meadow. Next time try saying the rhyme omitting the words: horn, sheep, cow, fast asleep, and crying. Instead, play the recorded sound effects for each omitted word at the correct time.

5. Utilize pictures, dramatic actions, and real objects, to depict the words: *blue, sheep, meadow, haystack, cow, corn, awake,* and *asleep.* Engage the children in a discussion about them. Rhyme and humor can be introduced by making some unlikely combinations of words. Were the sheep asleep? Was the horn in the corn? Did I cry? Can the corn blow the horn?

Grouptime Concepts: blue, horn, sheep, meadow, haystack, cow, corn, awake, asleep, humor, rhyming sounds.

Grouptime Skills: verbalization, memory, rhythm, sound discrimination.

Pattern 3

SMALL GROUP ACTIVITIES

1. MATH
Corn Measures

- Empty a large bag of unpopped popcorn into a dry water table, large dishpans, or mixing bowls.
- Place a tablecloth under the containers to catch spills. Give the children empty cans, cups, spoons, funnels, and bowls of different sizes to measure and pour with.

Concepts: empty, full, more, less, many, few.

Skills: scooping, pouring, estimating.

2. SCIENCE
Fresh Corn

- Cover a table or floor area with newspaper.
- Allow the children to shuck ears of fresh corn, while helping them identify the husk, silk, kernels, and cob.
- If possible, have some real corn stalks for the children to explore nearby.
- Pictures of cornfields and combines harvesting corn are also great language stimulators during this activity.
- When the corn is shucked, cut or break it into small pieces and cook in boiling water until tender.
- Let the children roll their corn lengthwise on a stick of butter, adding salt and pepper if desired.
- Eat and enjoy!

Concepts: ear of corn, husk, silk, kernels, cob, raw, cornstalk, inside of, on the outside of, cooked, boil, melt.

Skills: pulling, tearing, holding, rolling, observing, verbalizing, eating corn on the cob.

3. SENSORY
Blue Finger-painting

- Use blue-finger paint on a variety of surfaces such as: foil, construction paper, finger-painting paper, styrofoam trays, cookie sheets and smooth pieces of scrap wood.

- For a variation in texture, add kernels of corn or pieces of hay to the paint.

Concepts: blue, bumpy versus smooth textures.

Skills: feeling, designing.

4. LANGUAGE
"Little Boy Blue" Book Reviews

- Provide children with glue and a variety of shapes and objects which depict parts of the "Little Boy Blue" rhyme: corn kernels, shredded wheat cereal (for hay) and construction paper shapes that have been cut out *(See Pattern 3)*.

- Give each child a blank book of stapled paper and let them decorate their pages with the provided materials.

- Ask the children individually to describe the pages of their book. Beneath each picture, write exactly what the child says.

- On the front of the book write a title, the author's name, and the date. Page numbers can also be added.

- Encourage the child to re-read the book and to share it with others. These books are *great* to use at storytime.

Concepts: books have titles, authors, and pages, what is said can be written down and read.

Skills: creativity, storytelling, gluing, describing, imagining, re-telling a story.

5. DRAMATIC PLAY
Down on the Farm

- Fill a large tote or empty water table with hay.

- Add toy farm animals and popcorn kernels.

- Encourage the children to create a farm like the one on which Little Boy Blue might have lived. A haystack can be made easily by tying the top of a small bundle of hay together.

- Accessories can be molded from playdough, pressing hay and corn into them for realistic effects.

- The addition of small shoe boxes and blocks may help spark the development of farm buildings and equipment, furthering dramatic involvement.

Concepts: haystacks, farm environments, animals and the sounds they make.

Skills: dramatic involvement, manipulation of objects to form a desired environment.

6. ART
Little Boy Blue's Horn

- Provide each child with a construction paper horn *(See Pattern 4)* and a variety of decorating materials such as: crayons, paint, glue and glitter, magic markers, paper stars, paste and wallpaper scraps, peel-and-stick circle reinforcers, and yarn pieces.

- After the children decorate their papers, roll it lengthwise into a funnel-type horn and glue it.

- When dry, let the children "call" for the sheep and cows through their horns.

Concepts: a piece of paper can be given a three dimensional shape, voices sound different through a "horn".

Skills: creativity, dramatic involvement.

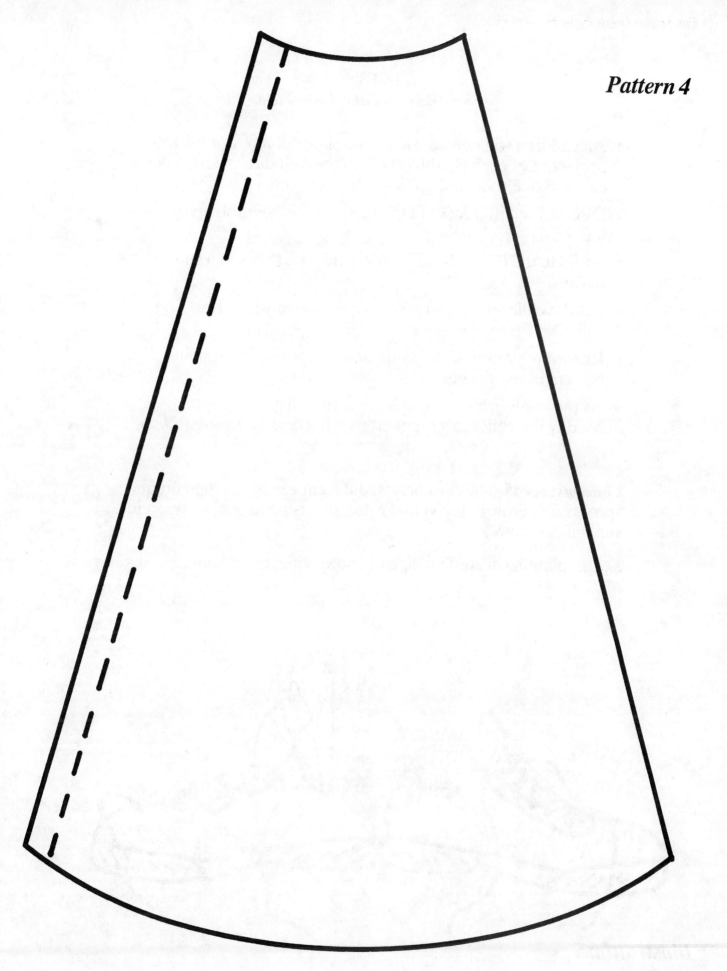

Pattern 4

29

7. SCIENCE
Shoe Meadows and Corn Fields

- All children will need a pair of old shoes of any size for this project. Let each child fill their shoes with dirt, planting corn seeds in one shoe and grass seeds in the other.

- Discuss the differences in the seeds as the children are planting.

- Sprinkle the dirt with water and place the shoes in a sunny place.

- Let the children predict which type of seed will sprout first and which will grow the tallest.

- Record their individual predictions on paper and tape it to the bottom of their shoes.

- As the seeds grow, compare the corn and grass sprouts. Modify the children's predictions if necessary. *(Illustration 5)*

Concepts: seeds grow into plants, different seeds produce unique sprouts and grow at individual rates, plants need dirt, water, and sunlight to grow.

Skills: planting, watering, digging, predicting, comparing.

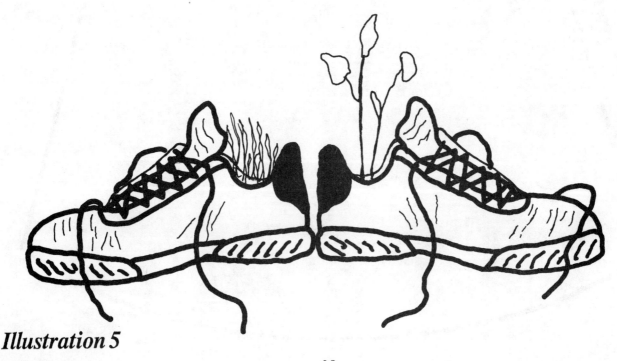

Illustration 5

8. NUTRITION
Cheese Haystacks

6 large shredded wheat biscuits

1/4 cup butter

1 cup grated yellow cheese

- Place shredded wheat in a doubled and secured plastic bag.
- Let the children crunch the cereal with their hands until it is finely crumbled.
- Meanwhile, melt the butter and cheese.
- Add the cereal to the cheese mixture and mix well.
- When the mixture is cool enough to touch, let the children form haystacks and place on waxed paper.
- Cool thoroughly, and enjoy!

Concepts: cooking, melting, haystacks.

Skills: crunching, mixing, measuring, shaping.

9. FINE MOTOR
Corny Playdough

- Give the children playdough and popcorn kernels to play with.
- Each child can mold ears of corn with the playdough and stick kernels of corn all over their "cobs".
- Some children might enjoy rolling their ears of corn over the popcorn instead.
- Tongue depressor "knives" can be used to cut the corn off the cob.

Concepts: cob, kernels, ear of corn.

Skills: fine motor control, manipulative skills.

MARY HAD A LITTLE LAMB

Mary had a little lamb,
Its fleece was white as snow;
And everywhere that Mary went
The lamb was sure to go.

It followed her to school one day,
That was against the rule;
It made the children laugh and play
To see a lamb at school.

And so the teacher turned it out,
But still it lingered near,
And waited patiently about
Till Mary did appear.

"Why does the lamb love Mary so?"
The eager children cry;
"Why, Mary loves the lamb, you know,"
The teacher did reply.

GROUPTIME ACTIVITIES

1. Sing "Mary Had a Little Lamb" to its familiar tune, adding a clap for each syllable of the repeating words. For example, on the first verse, claps would only be added on the words *"lit-tle lamb"*.

2. Use a toy stuffed sheep made with fake fleece to explain that the fleece on real sheep is wool, and that we use sheep's wool for clothing to keep us warm after it is sheared from the sheep. Show the children photographs in library books of sheep getting sheared. Liken sheep shearing to getting a haircut - it doesn't hurt and each sheep grows a new coat *(or fleece)* for the winter to keep itself warm. Bring in different examples of wool products such as: a sheepskin rug, fleece lined gloves or hat, sheepskin coat or vest, wool yarn, wool socks, or a wool sweater.

3. Invite someone who spins yarn to visit. Have them bring their spinning wheel and demonstrate the yarn-making process, from carding the wool to spinning the straightened fibers. The children will enjoy feeling and smelling the raw wool, too.

4. Using flannel pieces *(See Pattern 5)*, play a game of "Who's Following Who" on the flannelboard. Put up the flannel "Mary" first. Ask the children, "Where was Mary going?" *(to school)*; put up the flannel schoolhouse. Then ask, "What was following Mary to school?" *(the lamb)*; put up the flannel lamb behind Mary. Next place the cow behind the lamb. The cow is now following the lamb, and the lamb and the cow are both following Mary. Question the children as to "Who's Following Who?". Add the different animals to the flannelboard game, reinforcing the concept of following.

5. Encourage the children to hypothesize for a moment. The lamb's fleece was supposed to be as "white as snow". Could it have been as white as a marshmallow, a puffy cloud, cotton balls, or vanilla ice cream? What if the lamb's fleece had been pink? Perhaps it could have been as pink as bubblegum, a rose, cotton candy, or pink tennis shoes. Continue imagining colors that the lamb's fleece could have been, encouraging the children to use the simile "as *(green)* as a *(cucumber)*".

Grouptime Concepts: fleece, the wool we use in clothing comes from sheep, sheared, how yarn is made, following.

Grouptime Skills: singing with a group, clapping on cue, memory recall, hypothesizing, using descriptive language.

SMALL GROUP ACTIVITIES

1. SOCIAL STUDIES
A Visit to the Farm

- Plan a special trip to a farm which has sheep for the children to see. Springtime is a great season to do this because there is a good chance that there will be newborn lambs to observe.

- Try to arrange for the group to actually see a sheep being sheared.

- The children will want to examine the clippers that are used for shearing and feel the raw wool, after it has been cut from the sheep.

- If possible, bring some wool home for use in Activity 2, *Fuzzy Lambs.*

Concepts: lambs are young sheep, sheep live on a farm, sheep are sheared in the spring so that their wool can be used by humans, a sheep is not harmed by getting sheared.

Skills: observation, listening, questioning.

2.SENSORY
Fuzzy Lambs

- Cut out lamb shapes *(See Pattern 6)* from different colors of construction paper. If raw wool is available, make fuzzy lambs by gluing the wool on the paper lamb shapes.

- If wool is not at hand, cotton balls are a great alternative for this activity, and some added fun with color is possible.

- Make colored cotton balls by shaking white cotton balls in a plastic bag with a little powdered tempera paint. Make several different colors for the children to choose from.

- Encourage verbalization among the children concerning the texture of their pictures, offering words such as: puffy, soft, wooly, fuzzy, or furry if necessary.

- Write the children's descriptive phrases or sentences on their lamb pictures, reinforcing the grouptime concept of "as *(puffy)* as a *(pillow)*, or as *(white)* as *(snow)*".

Concepts: texture, colors.

Skills: gluing, using descriptive language.

3. GROSS MOTOR
Follow Mary, Follow Gary

- Have the children play this modified version of "Follow the Leader".
- Have the children build a structure to represent Mary's and Gary's school.
- Choose one child to be Mary or Gary, and have them lead the rest of the group to school.
- The leader decides the path to follow, which could be under tables, around chairs, or along the edge of a carpet.
- The leader also determines the mode of travel, whether it be hopping, crawling, or walking while clapping.
- When the group reaches the "school", a new Mary or Gary is selected.

Concepts: following, imitation.

Skills: gross motor skills such as hopping or jumping, following, imitating exactly what the leader does.

4. LANGUAGE
Fill in the Blanks

- Make a copy of the following story for every child.

- Help them each create a unique story by filling in the blanks, using the format of "Mary Had a Little Lamb".

_____ had a little _____, its _____ was _____ as _____. And everywhere that _____ went the _____ was sure to go.

It followed _____ to _____ one day, that was against the rule. It made the children _____ and _____ to see a _____ at _____.

And so the _____ turned it out, but still it lingered near, and waited patiently about till _____ did appear.

"Why does the _____ love _____ so?" the eager children cry. "Why _____ loves the _____ you know," the _____ did reply.

Concepts: changing a few words in a story can create an entirely new tale.

Skills: selecting new appropriate words *(i.e. nouns versus verbs)* to fill in the blanks, creative thinking.

5. MATH
Littlest Lambs to Biggest Sheep

- Make a Littlest Lamb to Biggest Sheep game board to introduce the concept of seriation, little to big or big to little.

- Cut two sheep of each size out of construction paper *(See Pattern 7)*.

- Using rubber cement, glue one set of sheep *(small to big)* on a large piece of poster board, adding such things as grass and a path with magic markers.

Pattern 7

- Protect the game board and the remaining sheep game pieces by laminating them or covering them with clear contact paper.

- Let the children try to match the sheep game pieces to the correct sized sheep on the game board.

- Introduce the concepts of small, smaller, smallest, and big, bigger, biggest.

- Talk about the fact that the smallest sheep are called "lambs," and that when they grow up they are called "sheep."

- As the children gain skill in matching the sheep, encourage seriation of the sheep without using the game board for reference. *(Illustration 6)*

Concepts: big, bigger, biggest, small, smaller, smallest, lambs are young sheep.

Skills: seriation with or without the aid of a game board.

6. SOCIAL STUDIES
It's Against the Rules!

- What are rules and why do we have them? What rule did Mary and her lamb break, and what did the teacher have to do?

- Get the children to respond to these questions in order to promote a discussion concerning the kinds of guidelines that we all live with daily.

- Examples of simple rules will probably come up naturally among the children. Write their ideas down on a large piece of butcher paper.

- Try to keep the list as positive as possible. For example, write, "Be gentle with other people" instead of "Don't hit."

- After a reasonable number of ideas have been generated, begin a "What If...?" game. Describe some different situations that deal with the listed rules, such as, "What if Susie hit Marian?"

- If it sounds as if a rule has been broken, the children can shout, "It's against the rules!"

Illustration 6

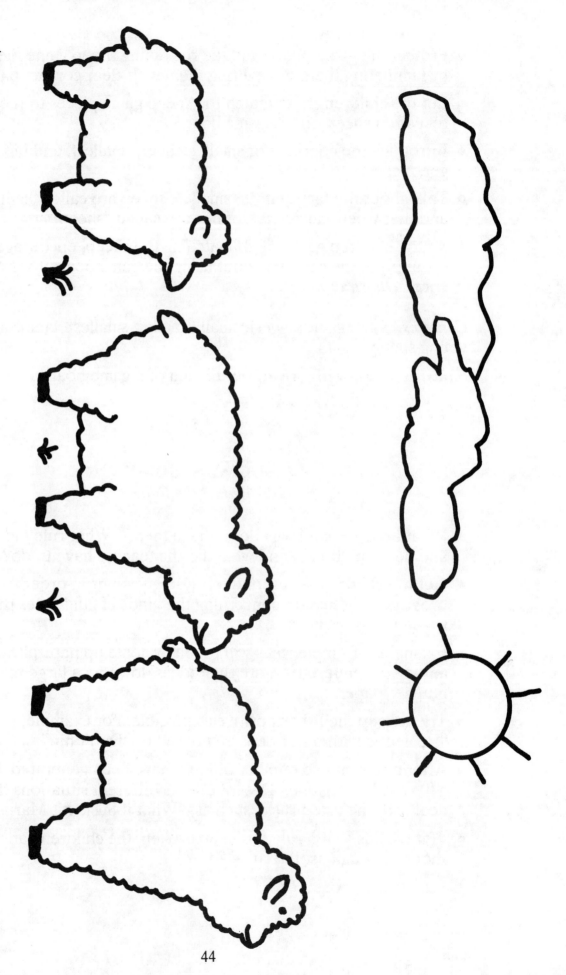

Concepts: rules are meant to be for the good of everyone, rules are for everyone to follow.

Skills: identifying familiar rules and actions that might break them.

7. FINE MOTOR
Snipping White as Snow Snowflakes

- Give each child a square piece of lightweight, white paper and a pair of safety scissors.
- Help them fold their paper diagonally to form a triangle *(See Pattern 8)*, and again two more times to make a small triangle.
- Let them cut random patterns out of the triangle, unfolding it occasionally to see the intricate patterns they are making from even the simplest cuts.

Concepts: Simple patterns multiply when cut out of folded paper, snowflakes are white, each one is unique.

Skills: Cutting, folding, unfolding.

8. ART
White Chalk Sidewalk Pictures

- Children love to use chalk to draw whimsical patterns and pictures on the sidewalk. The big, chunky sidewalk chalk is best for this purpose, because it isn't easily broken.
- Encourage the children to use white chalk to draw pictures of everything they can think of that could be white.
- Some ideas are: clouds, mashed potatoes, tennis shoes, cars, marshmallows, crayons, washing machines, lambs and snow.

Concepts: white, there are an infinite number of objects that could be white.

Skills: creativity using white chalk.

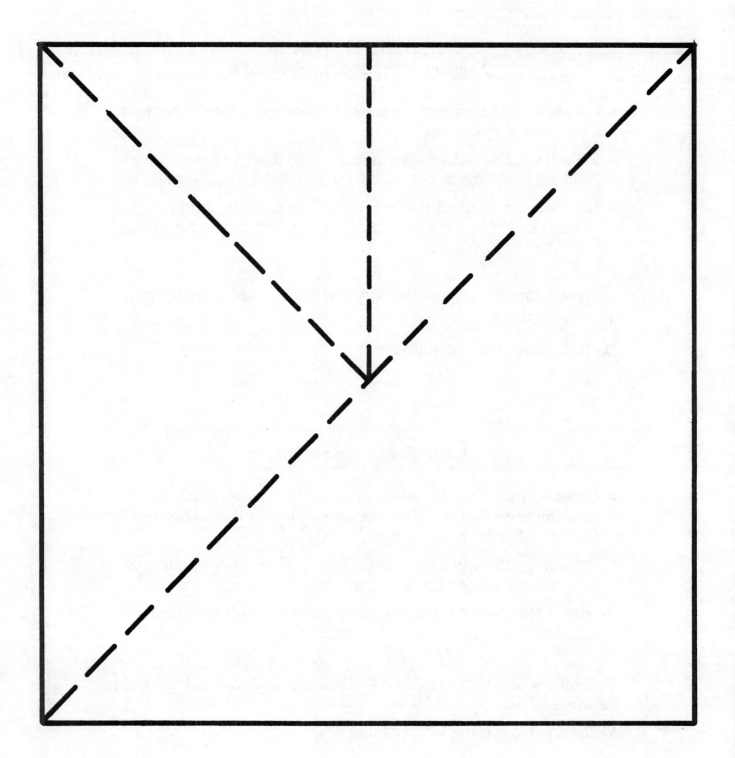

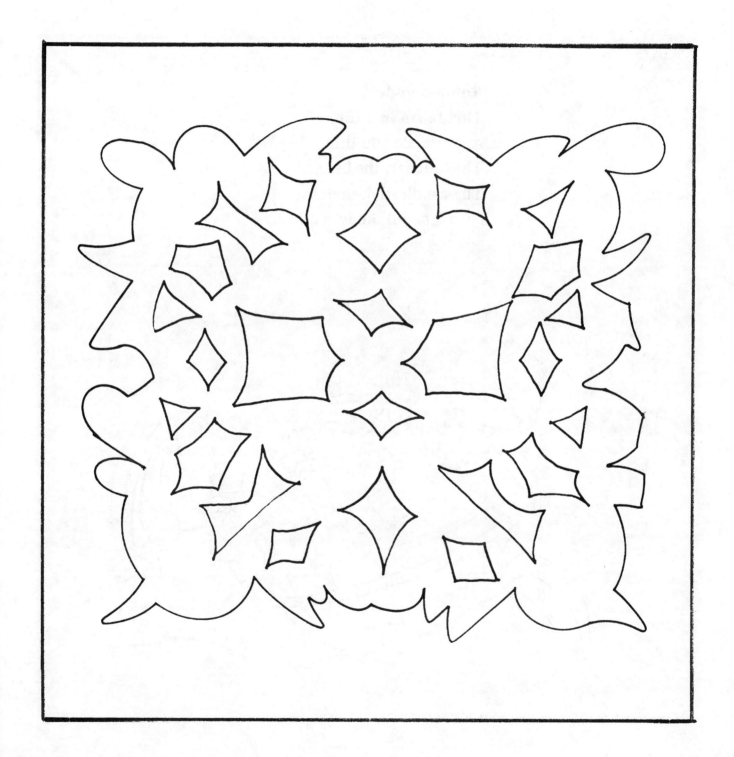

RUB-A-DUB-DUB

Rub-a-dub-dub,
Three men in a tub,
And who do you think they be?
The butcher, the baker,
The candlestick-maker,
Turn 'em out, knaves all three.

GROUPTIME ACTIVITIES

1. Read "Rub-a-Dub-Dub" aloud, while sharing an illustration of the nursery rhyme. Ask the children if they can tell which man is the baker in the tub. How do they know that he's the baker? Can they pick out the butcher and the candle-stick maker?

2. Play a simple game of "One, Two, Three, Do Like Me!" with the group. Explain that three is the special number in this game, because there were three men in the tub. Let each child have a turn demonstrating a motion for the group to do three times, in unison. The leader chants "One, Two, Three, Do Like Me!" while doing an action like clap, clap, clap, or twirl around, twirl around, twirl around. All of the children join in then, repeating the action three times together.

3. Have the children repeat the first two lines of the nursery rhyme: Rub-a-dub-dub, Three men in a tub. Now play a rhyming substitution game. Tell the children what the action will be that replaces Rub-a-dub-dub, such as Blink, blink, blink. Have the children say the new rhyme while doing the appropriate action, leaving the last word or phrase for them to fill in:

    Blink, blink, blink, three men in a *(sink, mink)*.
    Stomp, stomp, stomp, three men *(in a swamp)*.
    Tap, tap, tap, three men *(on a map, taking a nap)*.
    Ssh, ssh, ssh, three men *(in a bush)*.
    Knock, knock, knock, three men *(on a block, rock)*.
    Sit, sit, sit, three men *(having a fit)*.
    Stand, stand, stand, three men (in the band).

4. "Rub-a-dub-dub, you're going to jump in the tub! In this bag is everything you'll need. Try to guess what's inside."

In the sack there could be some shampoo, cream rinse, soap, a washcloth, a rubber duck, and a toy boat. Describe each object to the children by what it feels like, what color it is, how it is used, whether it floats or not, or what it rhymes with. Let them try to guess the name of the object.

5. Bring in a bag of objects that the Butcher, the Baker, and the Candlestick-maker might use. Let the children try to determine who might use what. Some of the things might be: *(for the baker)* a bread pan, measuring spoons, measuring cups, wooden spoon, *(for the candlestick-maker)* wax, matches, wicks, candles, *(for the butcher)* knives, cutting board, a food scale, white butcher paper.

Grouptime Concepts: butcher, baker, and candlestick-maker are all occupations; three; words can rhyme; objects can be grouped by where they're used or by who uses them.

Grouptime Skills: visual discrimination, repeating actions with a group in unison, combining actions with chanting, rhyming words, naming an object using verbal clues only, categorizing tools according to occupations in which they are used.

SMALL GROUP ACTIVITIES

1. NUTRITION
This Is the Way We Bake the Bread

- Make a simple baker's hat *(See Pattern 9)* for each child.
- Cut a headband from white construction paper, long enough to go around the child's head.
- Staple the ends together, forming a circle.
- Staple one side of a large piece of white tissue paper along one half of the headband.
- Poof the tissue paper up in the shape of a baker's hat and staple the other side to the headband.
- Let each child wear their baker's hat while baking bread.

Zucchini Bread

3 eggs	3 cups flour
1 cup oil	1 tsp. salt
2 cups brown sugar	1 tsp. baking soda *or*
1 T. vanilla	(3/4 tsp. soda high alt.)
2 cups grated zucchini	1 cup nuts *(opt.)*

50

- Combine flour, salt and soda; set aside.

- Beat the eggs. Add oil, sugar, and vanilla, mixing well. Add the zucchini.

- By hand, stir in the flour mixture just until moistened. Fold in nuts.

- Pour into two greased and floured bread pans. Bake at 350 degrees for 1 hour *(pyrex pans 325 degrees)*.

- Let bread cool for 10 minutes before removing from pans.

- Serve the Zucchini Bread for snack. For added fun, let the children keep their baker's hat on and eat by candlelight using the candle *(s)* from Activity 3.

Concepts: bakers often wear special hats, bread can be made from unusual ingredients - including zucchini.

Skills: Measuring, pouring, stirring, smelling, tasting something new.

2. MATH
Bakers' Measures

- Cover a table or floor area with a vinyl tablecloth.
- Fill several dishpans or large bowls with flour, salt, and sugar, and place them on the tablecloth.
- To add some interest, shake some colored sprinkles into one of the full bowls.
- Provide the children with a variety of baking props such as: measuring spoons, measuring cups, wooden spoons, spatulas, wire whisks, bread pans, cake pans, and bowls of all sizes.
- Watch the children concoct mixtures in their bowls as they invariably learn about empty, full, and half full.
- Help the children count the number of scoops of flour they dump in.
- Do they have more sugar or flour in their "cake"? Which pan has less in it? Can they add two teaspoons of salt to their "bread"? Which is heavier, the bowl or the pan?

Pattern 9

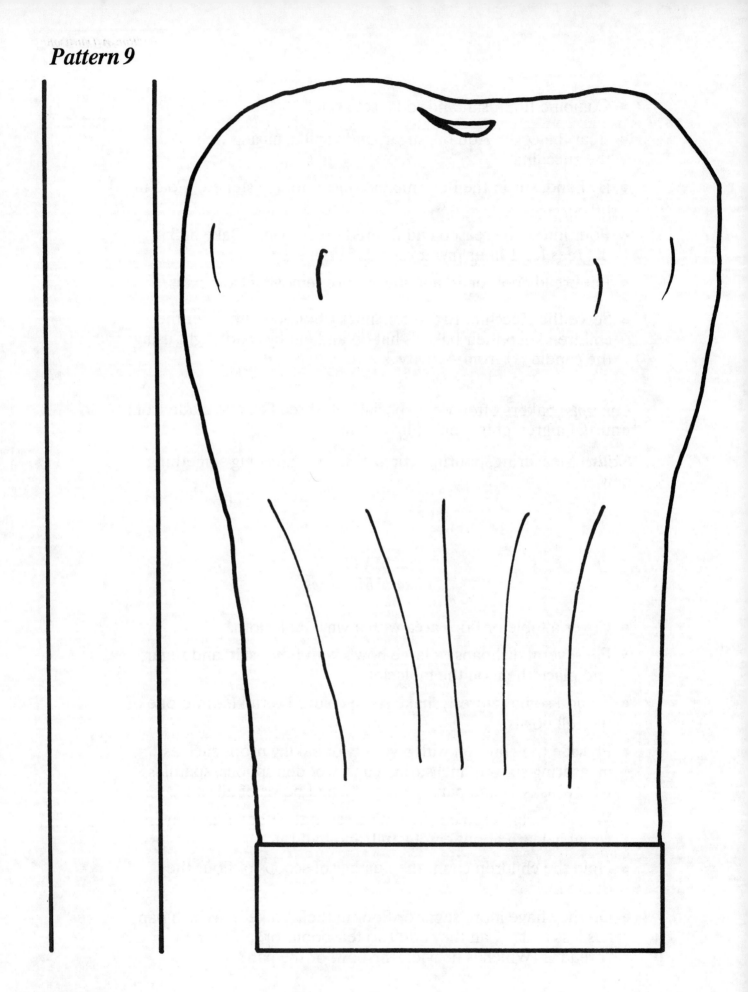

Concepts: empty, full, half full, heavier, lighter, more, less, bakers use many ingredients and implements to bake with.

Skills: measuring, pouring, mixing, counting.

3. SCIENCE
Candle Making

• Here's something for the adventurous soul with a well behaved group. Candle making can be a wonderful learning experience, but it does require great attention to safety. A crushed ice candle is particularly fun to make. It combines hot melted wax with a container full of cold crushed ice, to make a wonderful candle full of holes.

• Melt paraffin in an old pan, and add chunks of crayon to it for color.

• To make one big candle, cut the top off of a cardboard milk carton. Tie one end of a piece of candlewicking around a pencil and place the pencil across the top of the cut milk carton. The wick should hang down to the bottom.

• Fill the candle mold with crushed ice and pour the hot wax over the ice.

• Let the candle harden completely, then peel the carton away. Trim the excess wicking from the top and light it.

• If individual candles are desired, the same techniques can be used with small paper cups, with or without the crushed ice.

• After the candle making process is complete, encourage the children to recall the sequence of events they just observed.

• Make a group chart entitled "How Candles Are Made", listing each step as it is remembered. *(Illustration 7)*

Concepts: wax melts when heated, crayons dye the wax, crushed ice forms holes in the candle before it melts completely, candles have wicks, wax becomes hardened as it cools.

Skills: observation, recall.

Illustration 7

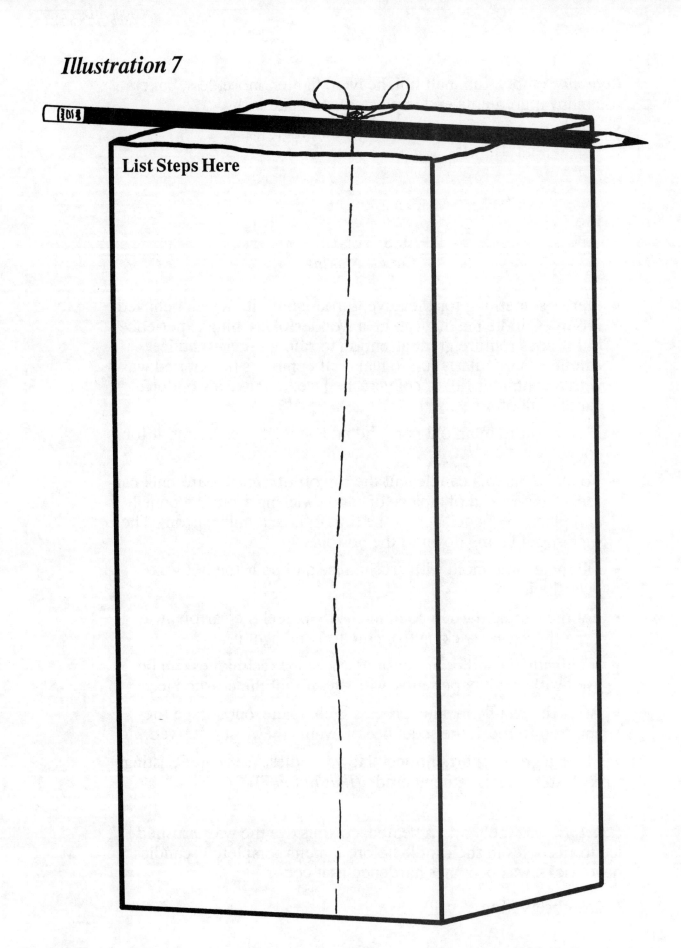

List Steps Here

4. ART
Crazy Candlesticks

- Each child will need a paper towel tube for this activity.

- Let everyone stuff their cardboard "candlestick" with some tissue paper in order to give it a little extra body during the creative process.

- The sky's the limit now. The point is for each candlestick to be as unique as possible, using whatever materials and techniques come to mind.

- Some ideas are listed below:

    1. Put glue all over the tube and roll it in glitter or colored rice.
    2. Use liquid starch to attach small pieces of colored tissue paper.
    3. Paint the tube with tempera paints.
    4. Glue on scrap pieces of fabric, ribbons, and trim.
    5. Use markers to make repeating designs down the tube.

- When the candlesticks are crazy enough, let each child stuff one end of the tube with some yellow and orange tissue paper, allowing it to protrude like a flame.

Concepts: candles have flames, candles can be one of a kind.

Skills: creativity, fine motor skill development.

5. SOCIAL STUDIES
Visiting the Butcher Shop

- Locate a cooperative butcher shop that would be willing to introduce children to what a butcher does.

- Give the ages of the children and explain that they will probably be full of questions.

- Ask exactly what the group will observe. Some interesting things to see are: the walk-in refrigerators, huge sides of meat, a meat grinder making hamburger, a meat slicer cutting bacon into strips, a bone saw cutting through meat with bones in it, butchers using knives to trim off fat, and the packaging of meat for sale.

Concepts: being a butcher is an occupation just as being a doctor or a bus driver is, butchers use many specialized pieces of equipment, butchers prepare meat for us to buy in the store.

Skills: observation, questioning.

6. FINE MOTOR
Meat trays

- Have the children cut out pictures of all kinds of meat from old magazines.

- Let them glue their pictures onto a styrofoam meat tray.

- Talk about the different kinds of meat the children have cut out, and identify their favorites.

Concepts: foods that belong in the meat category, often we buy meat that's pre-packaged on styrofoam trays, favorites.

Skills: Cutting with scissors, gluing.

7. DRAMATIC PLAY
Rub-a-Dub-Dub, Three Babes in a Tub

- Fill a large water table with warm water and a little bubble bath.
- Add three washable plastic baby dolls, empty shampoo and cream rinse bottles, shower caps, and some washcloths.
- Have dry towels and clothes for the dolls nearby.

Concepts: three; babies get clean by taking baths; the uses of shampoo, shower caps, and washcloths.

Skills: dramatic involvement.

8. SENSORY
Sudsy Finger-painting

- Squirt scented shaving cream onto a tray or cookie sheet and let the children finger-paint in the suds.
- If the tabletop is formica, the children can finger-paint directly on the table's surface, cleaning the table as they play!
- Encourage verbalization about the way the shaving cream feels.
- A word of caution, some children have very sensitive skin that may react to the shaving cream.
- Also, care should be taken so that no soap gets in the children's eyes or mouths.

Concepts: shaving cream is smooth, fluffy, creamy, soft, and smells great.

Skills: creativity, verbalization.

PETER, PETER, PUMPKIN EATER

Peter, Peter, pumpkin eater,
Had a wife and couldn't keep her.
He put her in a pumpkin shell
And there he kept her very well.

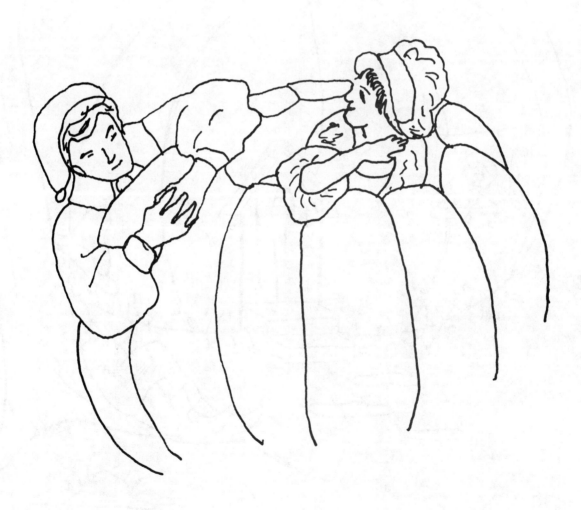

GROUPTIME ACTIVITIES

1. Read or recite "Peter, Peter, Pumpkin Eater" with a real pumpkin in view. Explore and examine the pumpkin with the children. Question them about ways in which Peter might have eaten a pumpkin. Did he eat it whole or cut up, cooked or raw? Did he bake it, boil it, or turn it into pumpkin pie? What is a pumpkin shell? Is it from the ocean like a sea shell? Can real people live inside of a pumpkin? How did Peter put his wife in a pumpkin shell? Draw a door and windows on the pumpkin and save it for Activity 2, *Making a Real Pumpkin House.*

2. Encourage the children to repeat the rhyme while doing a clap, knee slap rhythm. Then add a sing-song tune. Try saying the rhyme while marching, hopping, or jogging in place. Let the children dance and clap while reciting the rhyme with a syncopated jazzy beat.

3. Play a math game using a flannelboard with ten flannel pumpkins and a flannel "Peter and wife" *(See Pattern 10)* Use the pumpkins for counting fun as they are put up on the board. Then let Peter and his wife "eat" some pumpkins. Ask the children about the number they ate, and how many are left.

4. Use an overhead projector to demonstrate how yellow and red can combine to make "pumpkin orange". Out of colored acetate, which is available at art supply stores, cut two red pumpkins *(See Pattern 10)*, two yellow ones, and one each of any color other than orange. Arrange the pumpkins on the overhead projector and tell the following story:

   There was once the most incredible pumpkin patch ever to be seen. The pumpkins in this patch were all different colors. The pumpkin patch was very proud to be such an unusual group of pumpkins.
   One day they decided to combine their beautiful colors to make a rainbow. *(Move the pumpkins into an arch.)* It was then that the pumpkins discovered that they didn't have a single orange pumpkin in their patch. Their rainbow just wasn't complete without orange, but what could they do?

One yellow pumpkin said "Why don't you paint me orange so we can make our rainbow? After we make our rainbow, I can just wash the paint off." But the pumpkins didn't have any orange paint. It seemed like they would never get their rainbow finished! Then the red pumpkin called to the patch and said, "I've got the answer! Red and yellow make orange, so if yellow pumpkin and I just blend together we'll become orange!" *(Put an orange pumpkin on top of a yellow pumpkin.)*

The whole pumpkin patch was amazed that a little cooperation between two pumpkins could solve their problem. They were now able to make a beautiful rainbow, including orange, for the whole world to see.

5. Play the game "I'm Thinking of Something That's..." by verbally describing the following: pumpkin, stem, window, door, and orange. Let the children guess at the word being described.

Grouptime Concepts: pumpkins and their characteristics; number concepts; orange, red and yellow combined make orange, cooperation.

Grouptime Skills: hypothesizing, rhythm making, gross motor skills, problem solving, recitation, counting, subtracting, language comprehension.

SMALL GROUP ACTIVITIES

1. SOCIAL STUDIES
Visiting a Pumpkin Patch

- If possible, arrange a special trip to a pumpkin farm. There are often farms that cater to young children, offering tractor rides into the fields, attractive displays, and activities.

- Before leaving the farm, be sure to select several pumpkins for later use in other activities.

- If there isn't a pumpkin farm available, there may be a back-yard pumpkin patch nearby. "Backyard farmers" are usually eager to share their expertise with young children.

Concepts: how pumpkins are grown and harvested.

Skills: observation, listening, questioning.

2. SCIENCE
Making a Real Pumpkin Shell House

- Cut a pumpkin open at the top and let the children scoop out the seeds.
- Sort the seeds from the pulp and save the seeds for Activity 9, *Pumpkin Seed Outlining.*
- Discuss the parts of the pumpkin: seeds, shell, inside, outside, flesh, stem, and edible versus inedible parts.
- Talk about the parts of a house and cut them out appropriately.
- Save the pumpkin shell house for a centerpiece at snacktime.

Concepts: parts of a pumpkin, parts of a house.

Skills: scooping, sorting, verbalization, observation.

3. ART
Orange Magic

- Cut pumpkin shapes *(See Pattern 11)* out of yellow construction paper.
- Let the children paint the pumpkins with liquid starch.
- The pumpkins will turn orange wherever they have been painted with the starch.

Concepts: cause and effect.

Skills: painting, creativity, observation

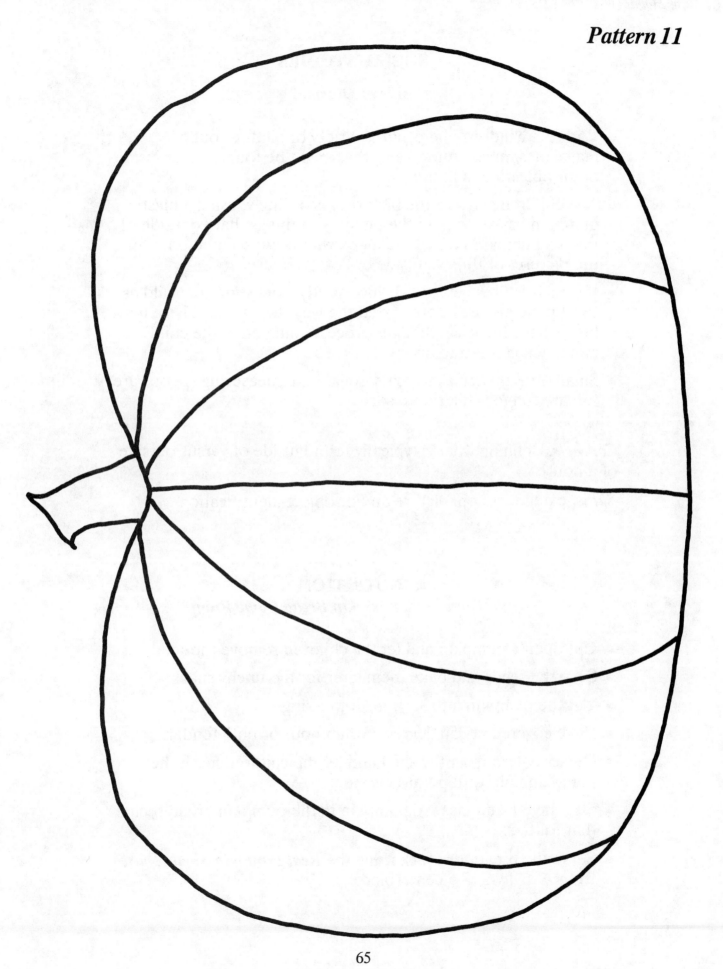

4. SOCIAL STUDIES

Inside or Outside?

- With the children's help, cut a variety of pictures out of magazines representing items that might be found either inside of, or outside of a house.

- The children can sort the pictures accordingly, using a plastic pumpkin basket to hold the pictures of things that go inside of Peter's pumpkin house, and a box with a sun painted on it for the pictures of things outside of Peter's house.

- If some pictures get sorted "incorrectly", question the child as to why the pictures were sorted the way they were. There may be a perfectly logical thought process going on in the child's mind, which is fun to discover.

- Small objects such as toy cars, socks, and measuring spoons are fun are fun for children to sort.

Concepts: defining what is typically found inside of versus outside of a house.

Skills: categorization, picture and/or object identification.

5. NUTRITION

Where Does Pumpkin Bread Come From?

- Cut open a pumpkin and let the children remove the seeds.
- Save the seeds and bake them later for a crunchy snack.
- Cut the pumpkin into sections for baking.
- Bake covered at 350 degrees for an hour or until tender.
- Remove flesh from the shell and let the children mash the pumpkin pulp with potato mashers.
- Use the cooked mashed pumpkin in the pumpkin bread recipe that follows.
- Serve the bread for snack using the *Real Pumpkin Shell House* from Activity 2 as a centerpiece.

Pumpkin Bread

1 3/4 cup flour	1/8 tsp. ground cloves
1 1/2 cup sugar	1/2 cup melted butter
1 tsp. baking soda	1 cup mashed pumpkin
1 tsp. cinnamon	1 egg beaten
1/2 tsp. salt	1/3 cup water
1/2 tsp. nutmeg	

- Sift the dry ingredients together.
- Combine butter, pumpkin, egg, and water, then add to the dry ingredients.
- Stir just until moistened and pour into a greased and floured pan.
- Bake at 350 degrees for 1 hour or until inserted toothpick comes out clean.
- Let cool for 10 minutes before removing from pan. Makes 1 loaf.

Concepts: inside, outside, flesh, shell, raw, cooked, where pumpkin bread "comes from".

Skills: mashing, measuring, pouring, stirring, scooping, and sorting.

6. LANGUAGE
We Made Pumpkin Bread!

- As a group, encourage the children to retell the sequence of making the pumpkin bread from scratch.

- Write their words on a large sheet of butcher paper and read it aloud with them when it is finished.

- Then let the children collectively draw pictures, on the butcher paper, about making the pumpkin bread.

- Record each child's statements about their drawing near their work.

Concepts: experiences and spoken words can be recorded by writing them down, drawings can also illustrate events.

Skills: recall, verbalization, creativity.

7. FINE MOTOR
Pumpkin Orange

- Cut styrofoam egg cartons in half (so that each child has six egg compartments), and remove the lids.

- Fill one compartment with red food coloring, one with yellow food coloring, and the rest with plain water.

- Give the children eye droppers to mix colors among the compartments.

- Also provide paper for the children to drop their pumpkin orange water onto. Paper towels are a good choice because it's fun to watch the color bleed into the paper.

Concepts: color identification, colors can blend to make new colors, liquid bleeding into paper.

Skills: creativity, use of eye dropper, decision making.

8. MATH
Which Pumpkin Is Different?

- Make "Which Pumpkin Is Different?" game boards out of poster board.
- Design these in varying degrees of difficulty to accommodate children of different abilities.
- The easiest board might have three identical pumpkin houses drawn on it, except that one house missing a door, or is a different color.
- A more difficult board might have five pumpkin houses on it that are the same, except that one is missing a stem. *(Illustration 8)*

Concepts: same and different.

Skills: classification.

9. EYE/HAND COORDINATION
Pumpkin Seed Outlining

- Draw a simple pumpkin shape *(See Pattern 11)* on a piece of construction paper.
- Let the children outline their pumpkin with glue and pumpkin seeds.
- Children also enjoy drawing their own shapes to glue pumpkin seeds onto.

Concepts: outlining.

Skills: eye/hand coordination, fine motor skills.

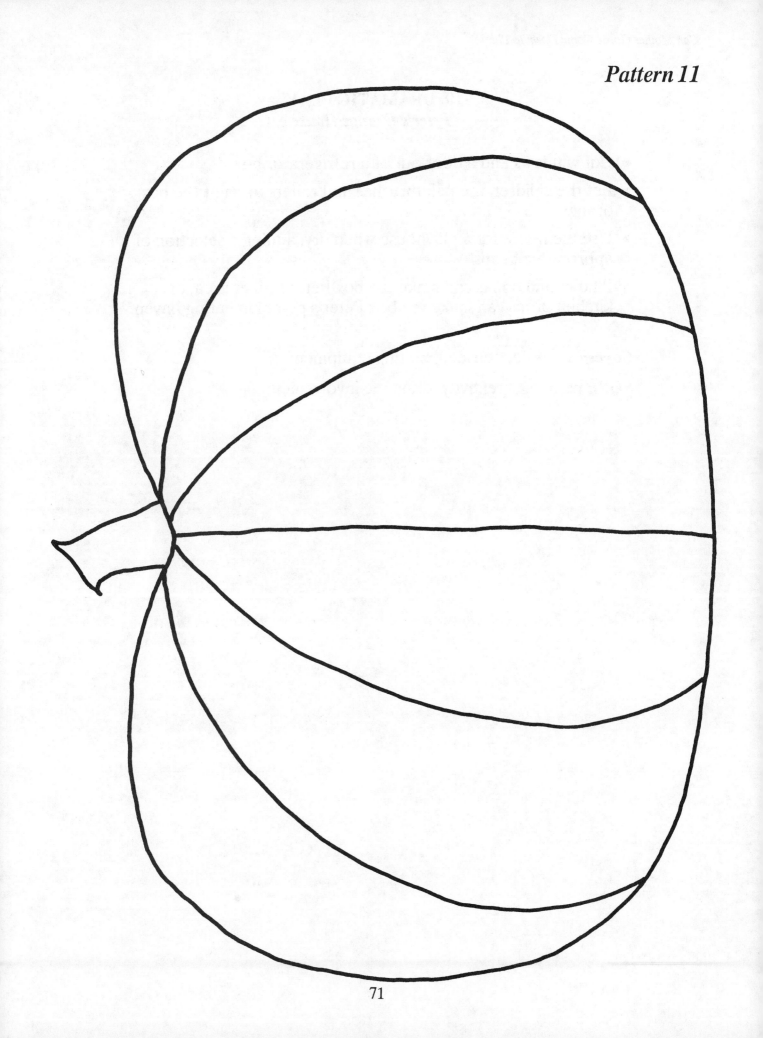

10. DRAMATIC PLAY
Peter's Orange House

- Cut windows and a door out of a refrigerator box.

- Let the children use paintbrushes and rollers to paint the box orange.

- Use the house for a playhouse when dry, adding a selection of appropriate props.

- Pillows and books can make the box Peter's quiet area, or kitchen props can make the box Peter's pumpkin eating haven.

Concepts: inside, outside, painting equipment.

Skills: painting, creativity, dramatic involvement.

HICKORY DICKORY DOCK

Hickory dickory, dock,
The mouse ran up the clock.
The clock struck one,
The mouse ran down,
Hickory dickory, dock.

GROUPTIME ACTIVITIES

1. With the children, sing or repeat the rhyme, "Hickory Dickory Dock". To help keep the group in rhythm, use a metronome, setting it to tick slowly at first, then adjusting the metronome to tick at faster speeds. Adding a few simple motions to the rhyme as it's being sung can make everything even more fun.

Hickory, dickory, dock, *(With straight arms, clasp hands and swing arms side to side like a pendulum,)*

The mouse ran up the clock. *(Run one hand up arm.)*

The clock struck one, *(Clap hands once.)*

The mouse ran down, *(Run one hand down arm.)*

Hickory, dickory, dock. *(Repeat pendulum motion. Say "Tick tock!" at the end, moving clasped hand back and forth.)*

2. Introduce the concept of telling time, using a large-faced clock. Move the hands so they read one o'clock, explaining that the small hand indicates what hour it is. Sequentially move the clock hands ahead one hour at a time so the children can grasp the idea of what time is displayed. If they seem to understand the hours in sequence, try mixing them up, but do keep it simple!

3. Using a tape recording of a ticking clock or a metronome, have the children clap their hands in time while saying, "Tick, tock, tick, tock." Then try stomping feet, tapping heads, or marching around the room in rhythm to the tape.

4. Why did the mouse run up the clock? What does it mean when a clock strikes one? Why did the mouse run back down again? Ask these and other questions to get the children interested in hypothesizing about the rhyme.

5. Display a picture of a grandfather clock. Talk about the parts of the clock: the face, the pendulum, the hands, and the wooden case. Explain that hickory is a kind of wood that comes from a hickory tree and it's sometimes used in making clocks. This could lead to a great discussion on types of wood that come from different trees. Bring in samples of many different kinds of wood for the children to see. Let them compare the weight, grain types, and colors.

Grouptime Concepts: slow, fast, telling time, parts of a clock, different woods have unique characteristics.

Grouptime Skills: singing in rhythm, singing while doing motions, telling time, hypothesizing.

SMALL GROUP ACTIVITIES

1.BLOCKS
A Grand Grandfather Clock

- Tape several pictures of grandfather clocks to the block area wall.

- Encourage the children to work together to build the grandest grandfather clock of all.

- Challenge them to construct an area for a paper pendulum to be housed.

- Help the children secure it in place, if necessary.

- Give them a cardboard clock face to finish off their structure.

Concepts: grandfather clocks are very tall, pendulums hang below the clock's face, the face of the clock is near the top.

Skills: cooperative building.

2. GROSS MOTOR
The Mouse Ran Up the Clock

- This simple activity is great for developing balancing skills for the participant and fosters group involvement for those waiting their turn.

- Elevate, at one end only, a sturdy plank or beam that's wide enough for children to safely walk upon. Be certain that the set-up is stable.

- Have the children begin chanting or singing the Hickory, Dickory, Dock rhyme while one child "runs up the clock" *(ramp)*.

- When the child gets to the top of the sloping board, the group should be saying, "The clock struck one, ..." and clap their hands once.

- The participant then turns around and "runs down the clock" while the rest of the children finish saying the rhyme.

Concepts: taking turns, up and down.

Skills: balancing while walking on a narrow, sloping surface, singing in unison.

3. DRAMATIC PLAY
A Mouse's House

- Drape a large old sheet over a table so it hangs down to the floor on all sides.
- Cut arched openings for mouse holes so the children can enter the mouse house.
- Make mouse ears *(See Pattern 12)* for the children to wear out of construction paper, stapling the ear shapes to the paper headband.
- Using an eye liner pencil, draw mouse whiskers and a black nose on the children's faces.
- Let the children color pictures to hang in their mouse house, using tape or safety pins to hang the pictures up.
- Save the mouse ears for use in Activity 7, *A Cheese Party For Mice Only.*

Concepts: mice and people have different facial features, mice usually like to hide away from people, pictures can decorate the walls of a house.

Skills: dramatic involvement, creativity in drawing.

4. SCIENCE
Tick Tock Clocks

- Clocks are made in all different shapes, styles, and sizes. Provide a table full of a wide variety of clocks for the children to explore.

- Consider digital clocks; alarm clocks with bells, buzzers, music or tweets; watches with numbers or dots on the face for hours; divers' watches; broken watches; mantle clocks; cuckoo clocks; clocks with pendulums or other visible moving parts; stop watches; ticking timers; hourglasses; and sundials.

- Talk about time and timepieces with the children. What time do they get up or go to bed? Help them set a clock of their choice to show these times.

- Using a clock, discuss units of time including seconds, minutes, and hours. What time is it right now? Do all the clocks show the same time? How do all these timepieces work? Do they use batteries, electricity, are they self-winding (using the motion of the wearer's arm), or does someone need to wind them? How are the alarms set? Using a stopwatch, how many seconds does it take to say the alphabet?

- Encourage the children to observe, question, and explore.

Concepts: watches and clocks "keep" time, timepieces have different styles, functions and means of operation; units of time.

Skills: questioning, observation, verbalization, comparing, contrasting, simple time telling.

5. EYE/HAND COORDINATION
A Mouse in the Cheese

- Cut out a piece of Swiss cheese and a mouse *(See Pattern 13)* from poster board and color them as desired.

- Punch a hole in the mouse and in the cheese.

- Tie one end of an 18" piece of yarn through the hole in the mouse, and the other end through the punched hole in the cheese.

- Let the children lace the mouse through all of the big holes in the Swiss cheese.

Concepts: mice love cheese, even with holes!

Skills: lacing.

6. MATH
Dozens of Mice

- Cut out dozens of mice *(See Pattern 13)* from gray construction paper.

- Staple on yarn tails and with markers add eyes, noses and whiskers, if desired.

- Hide the mice around the room.

- Set an alarm clock or timer for two minutes and tell the children to find as many mice as they can in that period of time.

- After the time is up, count the mice the group has collected.

- Introduce the concept of one dozen being twelve objects.

- Count the mice into piles of twelve and see how many dozen mice were found.

- Show the children a clock and count the hours together, noting that there are a dozen numerals on the face.

Concepts: one dozen.

Skills: counting, grouping by dozens.

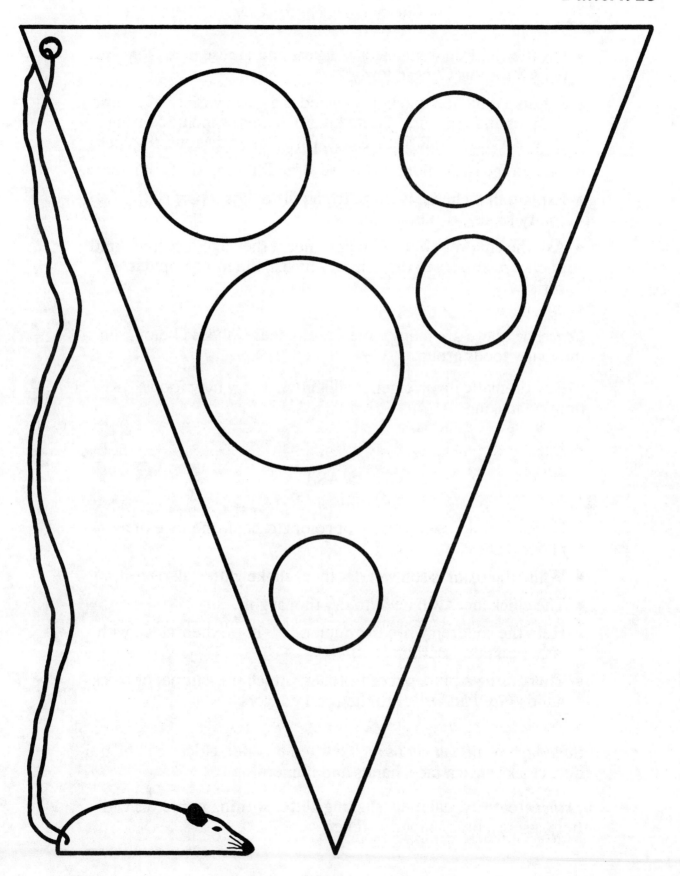

7. NUTRITION
A Cheese Party For Mice Only

- Let the children wear their whiskers and mouse ears from Activity 3 for this Cheese Party.

- Set up a table for snack that includes a good variety of cheese samples and crackers. Some favorite cheeses include String cheese, Colby, American, Swiss, Cheddar and Monterey Jack.

- Encourage the children to try several different kinds of cheese.

- Explain that cheese is made from milk and is a part of the "dairy foods" group.

- Ask the children to raise their hands if they like a certain kind of cheese and try to determine which is the most popular variety.

Concepts: there are many varieties of cheese, cheese belongs in the Dairy foods group.

Skills: dramatic involvement, willingness to try new foods, opinion making.

8. ART
Sparkling Clocks

- Let each child use a variety of colors to paint the face of a paper plate.

- While the paint is still wet, let them shake glitter all over it.

- The clock faces will need to dry thoroughly.

- Help the children write the numerals 1-12 on their clock with either paint or markers.

- Then, using a brass paper fastener, attach pre-cut paper clock hands *(See Pattern 14)* to the finished clock.

Concepts: paint can act as a glue when it is wet, clocks can be unique, clocks have a face, hands and numerals.

Skills: creativity, painting, shaking glitter, writing numerals with help, using a brass paper fastener.

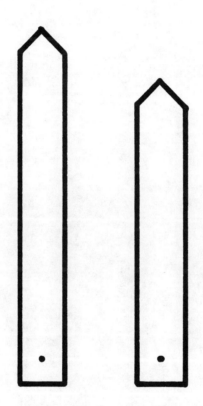

HUMPTY DUMPTY

Humpty Dumpty sat on a wall,
Humpty Dumpty had a great fall.
All the king's horses,
And all the king's men,
Couldn't put Humpty together again.

GROUPTIME ACTIVITIES

1. Recite "Humpty Dumpty" with the children while showing them a colorful illustration of the nursery rhyme. Encourage speculation as to why the king's horses and men couldn't patch up Humpty with a few bandages.

2. Create a "Humpty Dumpty Re-enactment". Build Humpty's wall out of blocks or use a table edge. Then cover the floor with a plastic tablecloth below the "wall". Place Humpty (a raw egg, complete with marker face and felt cut-out clothes, if desired) on the wall and ask the children to predict what will happen when Humpty takes his big fall. Then give Humpty a push and watch the reactions!

   Repeat the entire procedure, including the children's predictions, but this time make Humpty hard boiled. When the egg doesn't make the same splat on the floor, try to get the children to figure out why. Encourage them to feel and squeeze the egg if necessary.

3. Put several white flannel eggs of different sizes *(See Pattern 15)* up on the flannelboard. Discuss their oval shape and from where the eggs might have come. Introduce the concept of oviparous animals, which lay eggs. Chickens are obviously oviparous, but include animals such as lizards, turtles, crocodiles, barn owls, and ostriches in the discussion.

4. Read the books *Seven Eggs*, by Meredith Hooper (Harper & Row, 1985), and *Chickens Aren't The Only Ones*, by Ruth Heller (Grosset & Dunlap, 1981), to the children. They are perfectly suited to enhance the idea that all eggs don't come from chickens, and all animals that produce eggs are classified as oviparous.

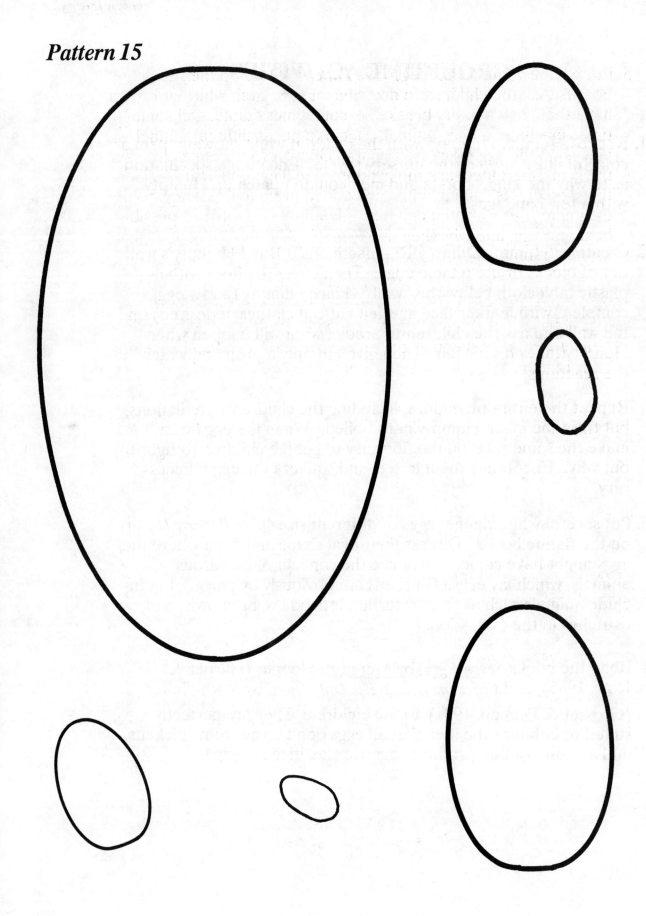

5. Put a large white flannel egg *(See Pattern 16)* up on the flannel-board. Ask the children to describe an egg: oval, white or brown, hard shell, usually very breakable, sometimes edible, and sometimes produces a baby animal. Begin to put additional flannel pieces on the egg to create Humpty Dumpty *(See Pattern 16)*. As the arms are added, ask the children if real eggs have arms. Continue on in this fashion with each added piece until Humpty is complete. Now ask the children if Humpty Dumpty can possibly be a real egg, and why they think so. Explain the concept of real versus pretend, if necessary.

Grouptime Concepts: broken, the properties of raw and hard boiled eggs, oval, oviparous animals, real versus pretend.

Grouptime Skills: speculation, prediction, categorization, listening, describing.

91

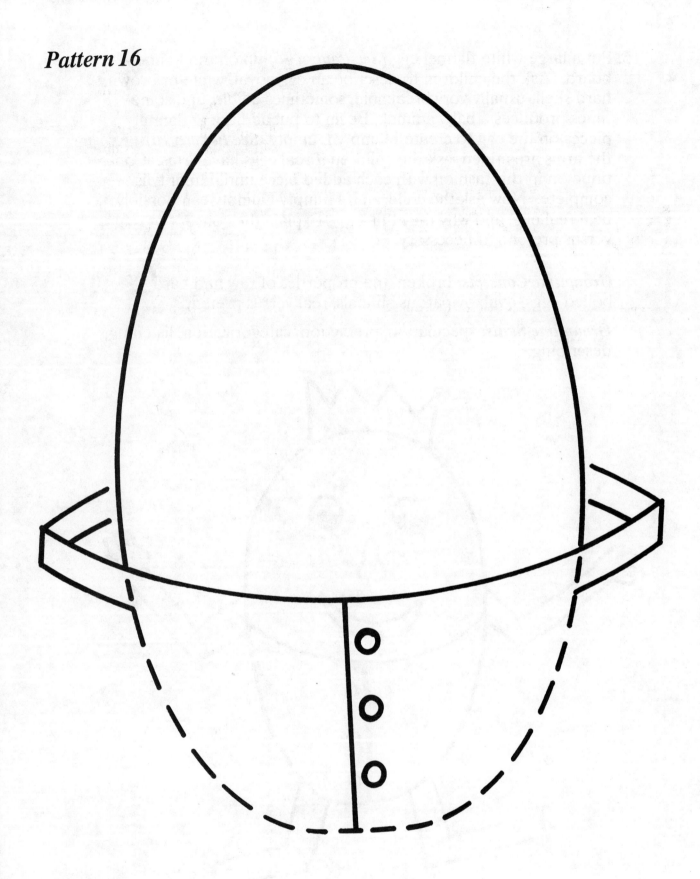

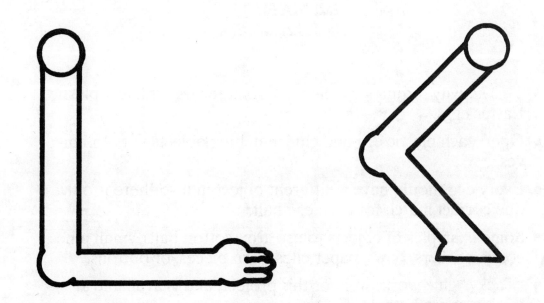

SMALL GROUP ACTIVITIES

1.ART
The King's Crown

- Using lightweight poster board, make a crown headband *(See Pattern 17)* for each child.

- Cover the crowns with aluminum foil.

- Let the children add "jewels" to their crowns by gluing on colored glitter, sequins, buttons, and beads.

- When dry, staple the ends of the crowns together to fit each individual's head.

Concepts: crowns are a part of a king's royal costume, crowns have jewels and beautiful decorations on them.

Skills: gluing, creativity, manipulation of small objects.

2. MATH
Egg Concentration

- This activity requires a collection of large large, fillable plastic Easter eggs.

- Open each plastic egg and glue matching objects in both halves.

- Every egg should have a different object in it so there is only one correct match for each egg half.

- Some examples of objects to use are: cotton balls, small pine cones, stickers, bows, paper clips, yarn pieces, or buttons.

- "Tacky" glue works well for this project, and is available at sewing or craft stores.

- To play "Concentration", take all the eggs apart, mix the halves up, and line out the egg halves upside down on the floor or table.

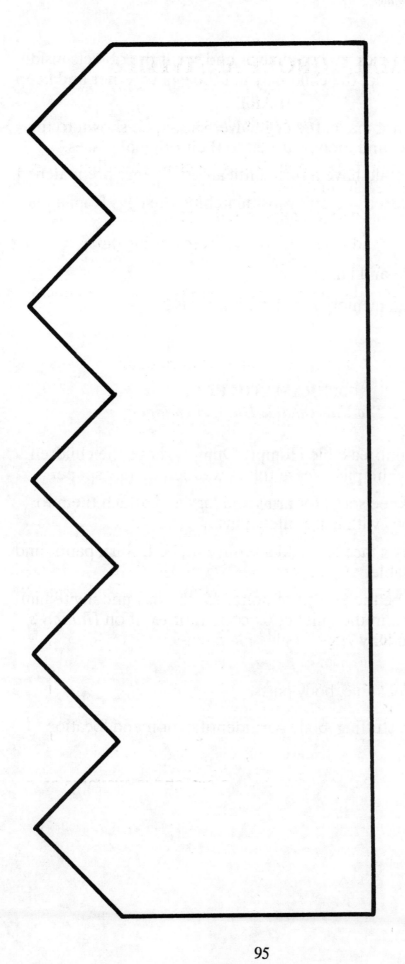

Pattern 17

- Let each child pick two egg halves and see if the objects inside match. If they do, the child may put the egg together and keep it.

- If a match is not made, the egg halves should be shown to the other children and then returned to their original places.

- Let the next child have a turn, until all of the eggs are matched.

- Younger children will enjoy just matching the eggs from a pile on the floor.

Concepts: whole and half.

Skills: matching, memory recall, taking turns.

3. DRAMATIC PLAY
The Unbreakable Humpty Dumpty

- To make an unbreakable Humpty Dumpty, have the children stuff an old white pillow case full of wadded up newspaper.

- Use stuffed knee socks for arms and legs and attach them to Humpty's body with large safety pins.

- Paint Humpty's face and add a funny hat, belt, shirt, pants, and shoes if available.

- Let Humpty be the person of honor for the day and invite him to snack, to sit in the quiet book corner, or to sit on *Humpty's Wall* from Activity 7.

Concepts: unbreakable, body parts.

Skills: wadding, stuffing, body part identification and location.

4. FINE MOTOR
Humpty Dumpty Cut-outs

- Using a broad-tipped magic marker on construction paper, draw a large oval shape and four 8" parallel lines about 3/4" apart *(See pattern 18)*.

- Let each child cut out an oval Humpty shape, and his arms and legs.

- The arms and legs can each be folded accordion-style, and then glued in place on Humpty's body.

- The children can add facial features and clothing, using crayons or markers.

Concepts: flat paper can be transformed into a three dimensional object, ovals.

Skills: cutting on straight and curved lines, folding, gluing, drawing.

5. NUTRITION
Edible Eggs

- Bring two pans of water to a full boil.

- Ask the children what they think might happen if whole raw eggs were placed into the boiling water.

- Have them speculate as to what the fate of a raw egg cracked into the water without its shell might be.

- In one pan, hard boil at least one egg per person.

- Crack a raw egg into the second pan.

- While the other eggs cook normally, let the children observe the raw egg boiling in the water and encourage the use of descriptive language.

- Remove the egg with a slotted spoon and place in a bowl.

- When the other eggs are hard boiled, cool them thoroughly in cold water.

Pattern 18

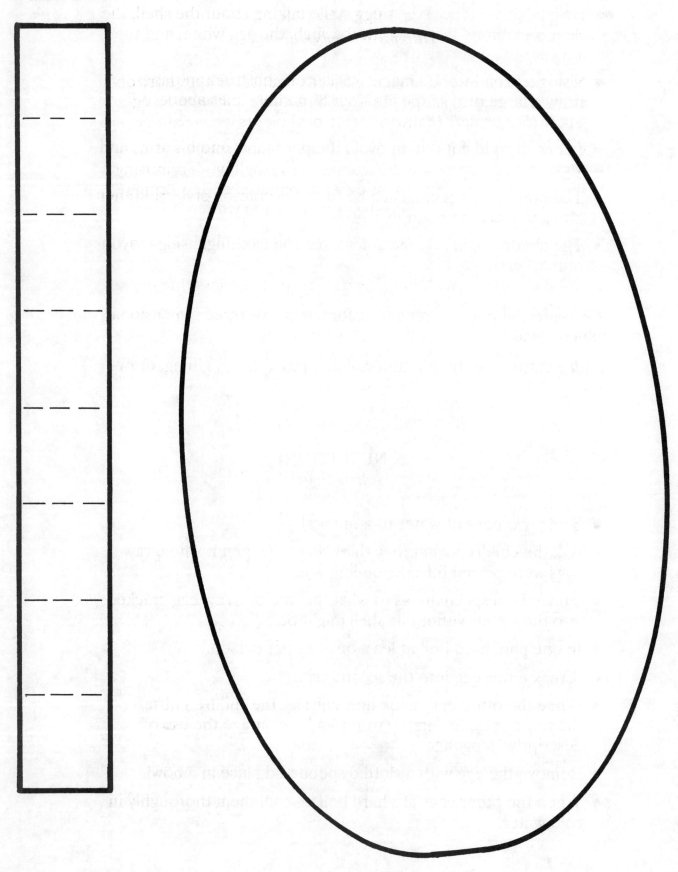

- Help each child peel their egg while talking about the shell, the clear membrane just beneath the shell, the egg white, and the not yet visible yellow yolk.

- Now get creative! Use an egg slicer to cut some eggs horizontally, then arrange all of the slices in a circle. Slice some eggs lengthwise or diagonally to create oval pieces which can be placed in an oval shape.

- Make deviled eggs by cutting some eggs lengthwise, removing the yolks and mashing them with mayonnaise, and returning the yolk mixture back into the remaining egg white.

- Create egg salad by mashing a whole egg with mayonnaise and a little bit of mustard.

- Cut some eggs into wedges by quartering them lengthwise and arrange the pieces in a star.

- Encourage the children to sample the different eggs, and to compare them visually to the one egg that was boiled without its shell.

Concepts: raw versus boiled, peeled, unpeeled, circles, ovals, shell, membrane, egg white, yolk, hard boiled, whole, half, quartered.

Skills: Prediction, observation, verbalization, tasting eggs prepared in different ways, comparing.

6. GROSS MOTOR
Hope Humpty Doesn't Dump Race

- This is the classic egg-and-spoon relay race, with a slight twist. Definitely use either hard boiled or plastic eggs!

- Construct a simple obstacle course for each team, including such things as: low block "walls" to step over, a winding masking tape path to follow, a table "bridge" to go under, or a trash can "tree" to go around.

- Gear the course difficulty to the abilities of the children.

- Give each team a Humpty egg, a large spoon to hold him, and let the race begin!

Concepts: team effort, taking turns.

Skills: coordination, balance, following an outlined course.

7. BLOCKS
Humpty's Wall

- Place *The Unbreakable Humpty Dumpty* from Activity 3 in the block building area.

- Encourage the children to cooperate in building a tall, but sturdy wall for Humpty to really sit on.

- Demonstrate a typical staggered brick laying pattern with the blocks.

- Give each child a plastic egg filled with several white cotton balls and one yellow cotton ball (for the egg white and yolk).

- The "yolks" can easily be made by shaking white cotton balls in a little yellow powdered tempera paint.

- Challenge each child to build a brick wall for their egg, which will keep it from falling and cracking open.

Concepts: cooperation, strength and function in design, brick laying pattern.

Skills: problem solving, block building.

8. SCIENCE
Which Egghead's Ahead?

- Let each child make an "Egghead", using magic markers on a plastic, fillable egg.

- Let them scout the room for some small object(s) to put in their eggs.

- Set up a ramp that the children can roll their "Eggheads" down, or use thc playground slide.

- Before the children race their eggs, ask the group for predictions as to which egg will roll the fastest.

- After the races, have the children show each other what's inside their egg.

- Try to help the children discover that the egg with the heaviest object(s) inside, will roll the fastest, provided they are not pushed!

- Let the children change the objects inside of their eggs, and have an "Egghead Re-Match".

Concepts: an object's weight influences its speed when rolled down a ramp.

Skills: prediction, ability to modify "design" after gaining new knowledge.

THREE LITTLE KITTENS

Three little kittens,
They lost their mittens,
And they began to cry,
"Oh, mother dear, we sadly fear
Our mittens we have lost."

"What! Lost your mittens?
You naughty kittens!
Then you shall have no pie."
"Meow, meow, meow."
"No, you shall have no pie."

The three little kittens,
They found their mittens,
And they began to cry,
"Oh, mother dear, see here, see here,
Our mittens we have found."

"What! Found your mittens?
You silly kittens!
Then you shall have some pie."
"Purr-r, purr-r, purr-r,
Oh, let us have some pie."

The three little kittens,
Put on their mittens,
And soon ate up the pie;
"Oh, mother dear, we greatly fear
Our mittens we have soiled."

"What! Soiled your mittens?
You naughty kittens!"
Then they began to sigh,
"Meow, meow, meow."
Then they began to sigh.

The three little kittens,
They washed their mittens,
And hung them out to dry;
"Oh, mother dear, look here, look here.
Our mittens we have washed."

"What! Washed your mittens?
You're good little kittens,
But I smell a rat close by!
Hush! Hush! Hush!
I smell a rat close by."

GROUPTIME ACTIVITIES

1. There are several versions of *The Three Little Kittens* in book form, that are available in children's libraries. These books will portray the rhyme more richly than is possible when it's included in a Mother Goose collection. Select an illustrator's work whose pictures are particularly enjoyable, and share it with the children.

2. Ask the children to bring in pairs of mittens. Develop a representational graph on poster board, using paper mitten shapes *(See Illustration 19)* that shows their color and/or pattern distribution. Engage the children in a conversation about the graph. It can easily help explain the concepts of most, least, none, and how many. Are there more plain mittens or patterned mittens? How many blue mittens are there? Which color of mitten are there the least of? Display the graph on the wall so the children can go back to it later, individually.

3. Introduce the concept of a pair by using flannelboard pieces depicting three kittens, their three pairs of mittens, and three pairs of shoes *(See Pattern 19)*. Count the kittens, mittens, and shoes. How many mittens does each kitten need and how many shoes? Organize the clothing into pairs for each kitten. Continue to improvise the counting, addition, and subtraction games as the kittens "lose" or "find" their mittens.

4. Play "Which Mitten's Missing?" Let the children study a tray displaying three pairs of real mittens. Cover them and remove a single mitten. Uncover the tray and ask, "Which mitten's missing?" As the children get better at this game, mix up the pairs or add more mittens to the tray.

Illustration 9

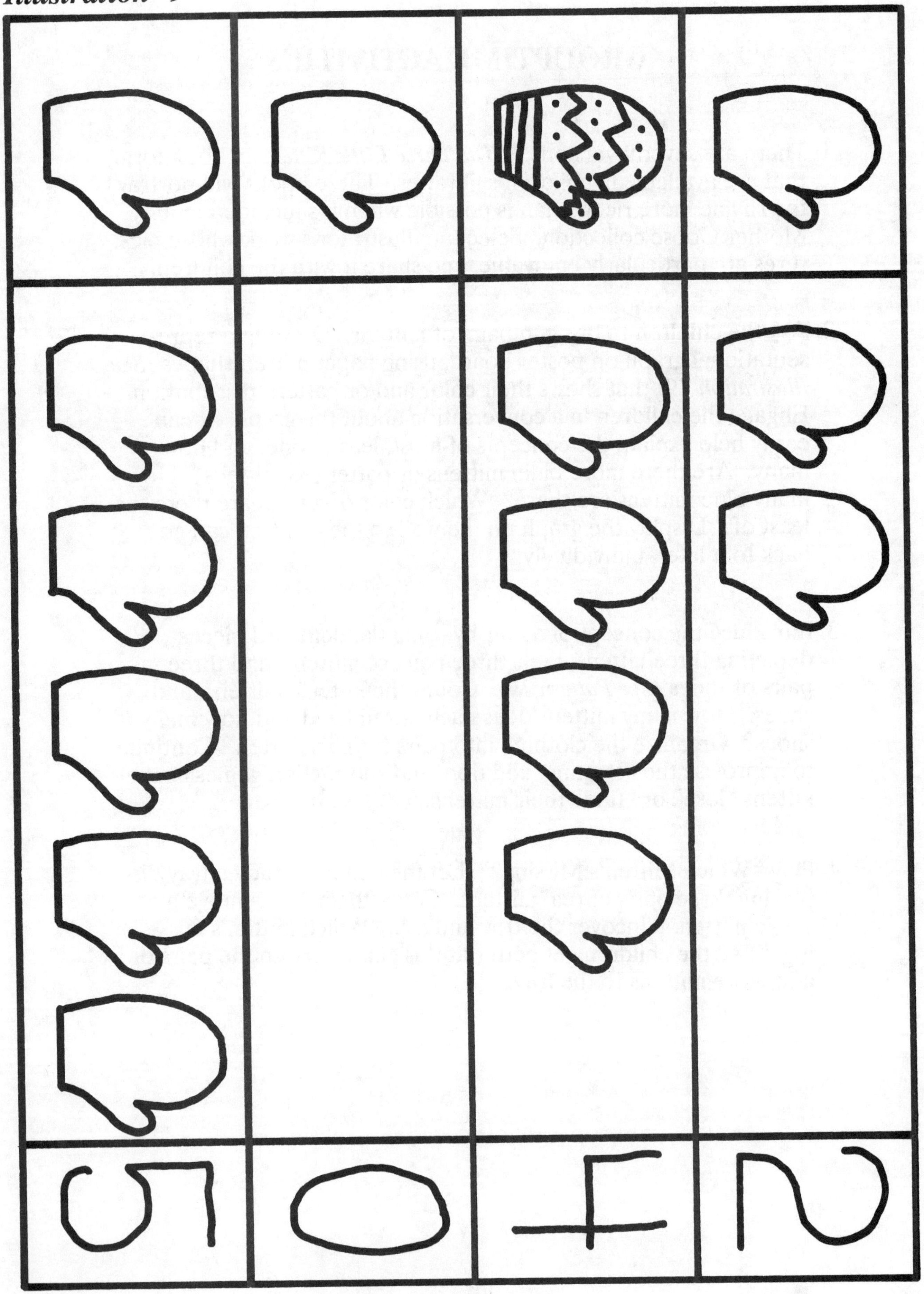

5. Call the Humane Society and ask them to visit the class with a kitten from their shelter. They usually have a trained person who specializes in visiting groups for educational purposes. Ask the representative to talk to the children about how to pet a kitten appropriately and what kind of special care a kitten needs. Encourage the children to listen, ask questions and to handle the kitten gently.

Grouptime Concepts: three, a pair is two, most, least, none, how many, representational graphing, a kitten's characteristics and needed care.

Grouptime Skills: categories, adding, subtracting, counting, visual memory, listening, questioning, observing, petting.

SMALL GROUP ACTIVITIES

1. SENSORY
Washing Mittens

- Fill a water table or large pan with warm sudsy water and have another tub of clean water nearby.

- String a clothesline between two chairs and clip some clothespins on it, with some towels on the floor underneath to catch the drips.

- Now the children are ready to wash and rinse their mittens, and then hang them up to dry.

Concepts: dirty, clean, wet, dry, soapy.

Skills: squeezing, scrubbing, rinsing, using clothespins.

Note: Duplicate Pattern 19

2. MATH
Mitten Sorting and Patterning

- Cut three kittens and lots of mittens *(See Pattern 20)* from three colors of construction paper.

- Encourage the children to sort the mittens by color, piling all of the red mittens on top of the red kitten, and the yellow mittens on top of the yellow kitten.

- Remove the kittens and line out a simple mitten pattern such as red, yellow, red, yellow.

- Ask what mitten should come next and see if the children can continue the pattern, or if they can make the same pattern using different colors.

- The children may enjoy coming up with their own patterns for others to copy, too.

- Introduce more complex patterns as the children's skills increase.

Concepts: same, different, patterns are repeating sequences.

Skills: color sorting, patterning.

3. EYE/HAND COORDINATION
Magnetic Mitten Fishing

- Cut lots of mittens out of colored paper *(See Pattern 20)* and attach several paper clips to each one.

- Make simple fishing poles by tying a magnet to one end of a string, and the other end of the string to a ruler or other short stick.

- Put all of the mittens in a large washtub and let the children fish for the mittens magnetically.

- "Caught" mittens can just be piled up, or color sorted if an additional challenge is wanted.

Concepts: colors, caught, magnetic.

Skills: coordination, patience, persistence.

4. ART
Pairs Of Mittens

- Provide the children with pre-cut paper mitten shapes *(See Pattern 21)*.

- Give them a variety of yarn, fabric, and leather scraps to cut and glue on to their mittens.

- Older children may enjoy the challenge of making a matching pair of mittens.

Concepts: mittens can be made from a variety of materials, pairs of mittens have two identical mates.

Skills: designing, cutting, gluing, making matching mittens.

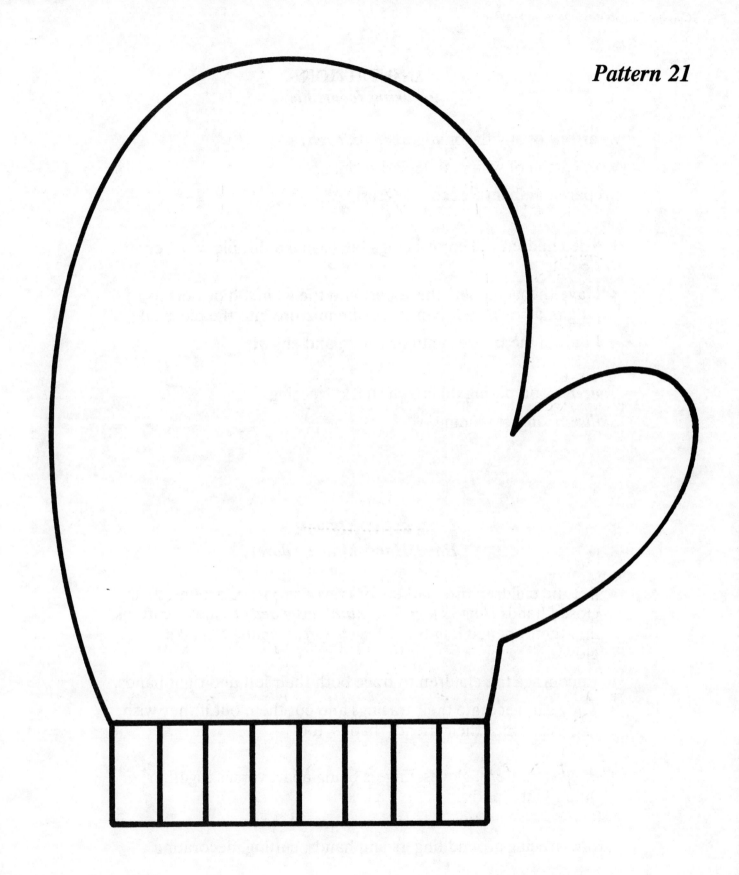

5. NUTRITION
Making Yogurt Pie

2 cartons of any flavor yogurt *(8 oz. each)*

9 oz. carton of whipped dessert topping

prepared graham cracker pie crust

- The children will enjoy being able to make this pie with very little help.
- Have them combine the yogurt and the whipped dessert topping in a bowl, and then scoop the mixture into the pie shell.
- Put it in the freezer until firm, cut, and enjoy!

Concepts: preparing their own snack, freezing.

Skills: mixing, spreading.

6. FINE MOTOR
Hand, Hand, Mitten, Glove

- Let the children use markers or crayons to trace around their closed hands *(fingers together, thumb extended)* to make mittens, and their opened hands *(all fingers spread apart)* to make gloves.
- Encourage the children to trace both their left and right hands.
- They can decorate their tracings and cut them out if they wish, and even trace their friends' hands, too.

Concepts: mittens, gloves, fingers being apart versus together, right and left hands.

Skills: tracing around fingers and hands, cutting, decorating.

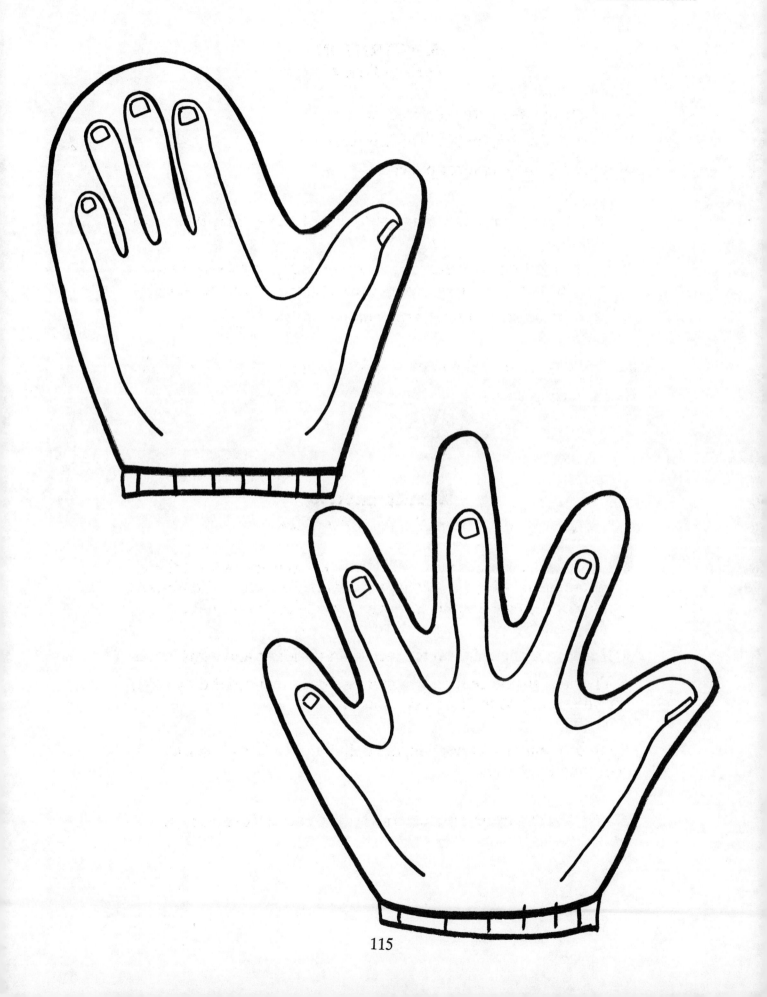

LITTLE JACK HORNER

Little Jack Horner
Sat in a corner
Eating a Christmas pie.
He stuck in his thumb
And pulled out a plum,
And said, "What a good boy am I!"

GROUPTIME ACTIVITIES

1. Use a puppet to act out the rhyme "Little Jack Horner" as it is read.

2. Draw happy faces on the children's thumbs. Repeat the rhyme together and dramatize it with hands by making an "L" shape corner with one hand and putting the thumb with the happy face on it in the corner. Make the thumb pull out a plum and nod while saying, "What a good boy am I!"

3. With happy faces on the children's thumbs, do the appropriate motions while chanting:

   > My thumbs go up, up, up,
   > My thumbs go down, down, down,
   > My thumbs go out, out, out,
   > My thumbs go in, in, in,
   > My thumbs go around!

4. Have the children make a fist and call it a plum. Use the happy face thumb from the other hand to put: thumb on plum, thumb in plum, thumb over plum, and thumb under plum. Then make the plum and thumb disappear and reappear.

5. Cut out five flannel plums and plum pits in seriated sizes *(See Pattern 22)*. On the flannelboard, have the children seriate the plums and plum pits from biggest to smallest. Then give each plum its corresponding pit. Repeat the activity, but this time seriate from smallest to biggest.

Grouptime Concepts: thumbs, up, down, out, in, around, on, in, over, under, disappear, reappear, biggest, smallest.

Grouptime Skills: oral recitation while doing finger plays, seriation by size, one-to-one correspondence, recognition of correct size relationships.

Pattern 22

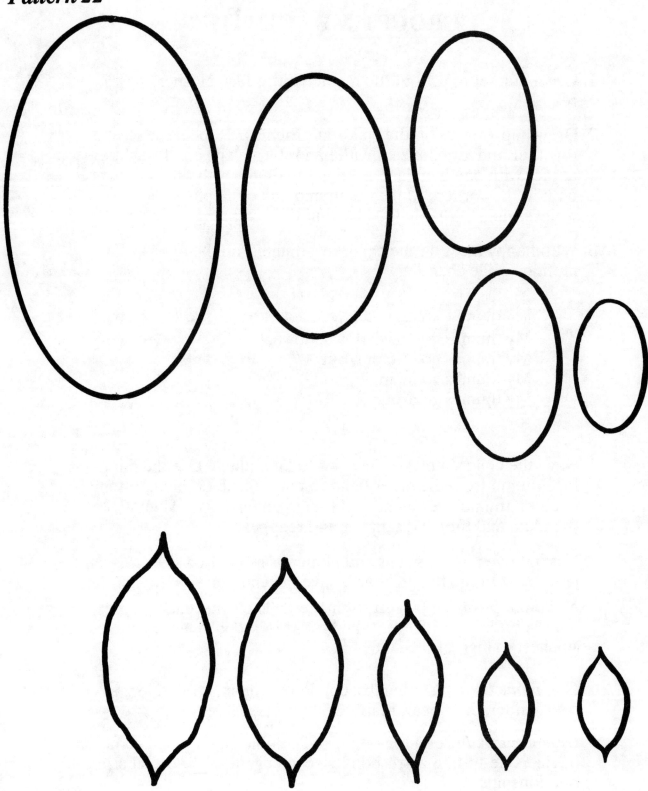

SMALL GROUP ACTIVITIES

1. MATH
Pie Puzzles

- Use four foil pie pans for the puzzle containers.

- Cut eight construction paper circles that are the diameter of the bottom of the pie pans, two each of brown, purple, red, and blue.

- Using a magic marker and a straight edge, divide each paper pie into pieces, but both papers of the same color should be divided identically.

- This is a perfect opportunity to introduce the concept of fractions: halves, quarters, thirds, and sixths.

- Glue one brown paper pie into a foil pie pan and cut the identical brown paper pie into the matching puzzle pieces.

- Finish the other pie puzzles the same way.

- Affix "scratch and sniff" stickers to the different flavor pies, if desired. *(Illustration 10)*

Concepts: part, whole, fractions, colors, flavors are typically identified by certain colors.

Skills: color and size matching.

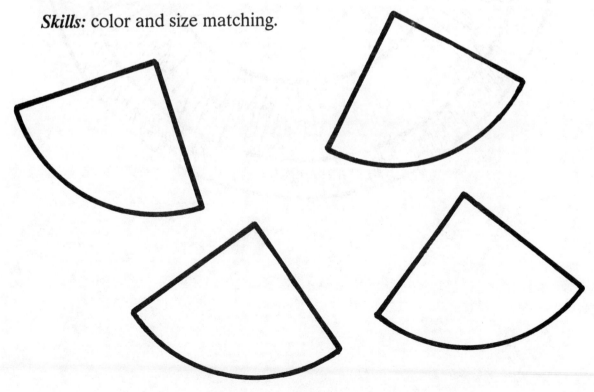

Illustration 10

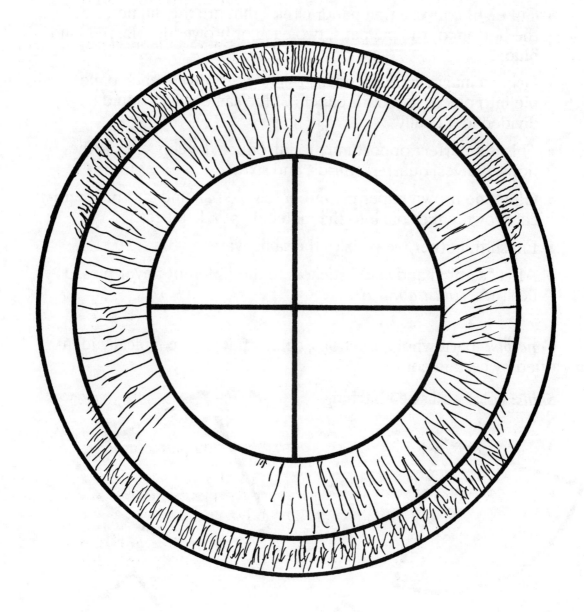

2. FINE MOTOR
Purple Paper Cutting

- Allow the children to cut randomly on purple paper of various sizes and shapes.

- Thin paper strips for snipping are fun for children at the fringing stage of cutting.

- For more advanced cutters, wide magic marker lines can be drawn to cut on.

- Begin with straight lines, adding curves and circles as the children's skills improve.

- Provide pie tins for the children to fill with the purple pieces they cut.

Concepts: purple, pieces, big, little, many, just a few.

Skills: cutting.

3. ART
A Thumb Plum Tree

- On a large piece of butcher paper, draw a simple outline of a tree.
- Tape the tree to the wall, table, or floor, and place dishes of purple paint close by.
- Let the children stick their thumbs in the paint and then onto the tree, making thumbprint plums all over the tree.
- This activity helps promote a cooperative, creative spirit among the children, as the resulting mural belongs to the group instead of an individual.

Concepts: plums grow on trees, plums are purple, thumbs can make thumbprints.

Skills: printing with thumbs, cooperative design.

4. NUTRITION
A Plum-Tasting Party

- Children always seem ready for a snack, so try introducing plums.

- If possible, have at least two fresh varieties to taste, as well as some dried plums *(better known as prunes)* and canned plums.

- Encourage the children to see if they can find the pits inside and to try all of the different kinds.

- Talk about the characteristics of the plums, their textures ,and colors.

- Later, plant the pits to see if they grow.

Concepts: plums are fruits, have pits, and are purple; plums can be purple or yellowish inside, prunes are dried plums.

Skills: tasting new foods, comparing, planting.

5. DRAMATIC PLAY
Making Christmas (Mud) Pies

- Add water to the sandbox to make the sand of good shaping consistency.

- Provide the children with foil pie tins and cooking implements.

- Aprons and baker hats *(See Pattern 9)* are also fun props.

Concepts: baking, full, empty.

Skills: pretending, dumping, filling, smoothing, verbalizing.

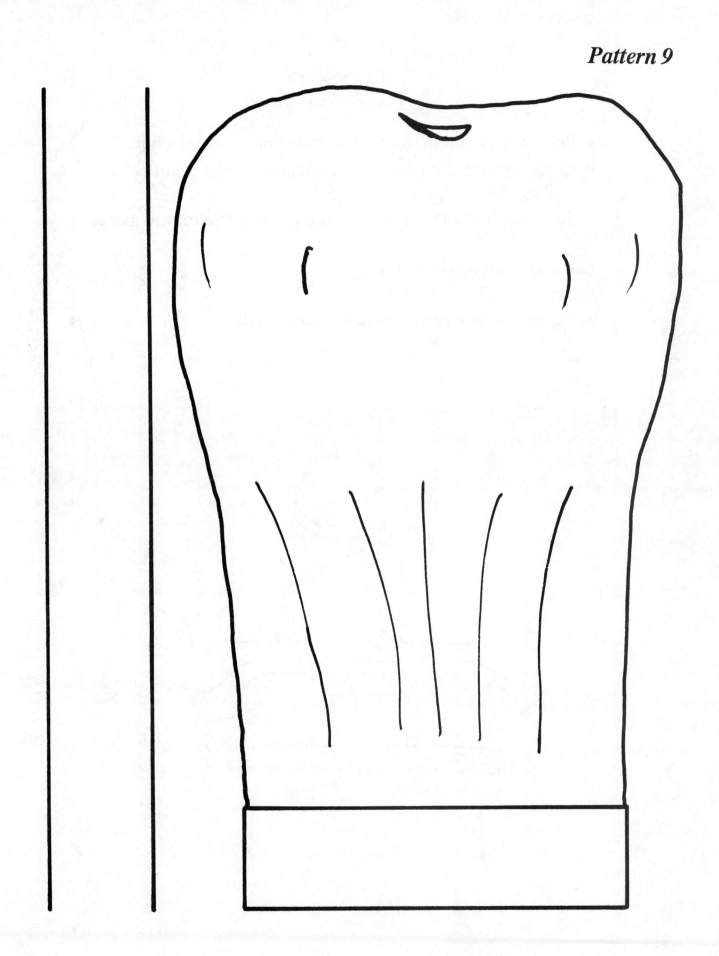

6. SENSORY
Fruity "Feely" Box

- Put a variety of fresh fruits, including a plum, inside a box.

- Cover it with a cloth and ask the children to find a particular fruit by touch only.

- Some children might also enjoy using a blindfold for this game.

Concepts: fruit names and shapes.

Skills: feeling as a method of object identification.

7. EYE/HAND COORDINATION
Stringing Plum Necklaces

- Cut out many construction paper purple plum shapes *(See Pattern 23)* for stringing.

- Punch a hole near the top in each plum.

- Give each child some plums and a piece of yarn with tape wrapped around the end of it for stiffness.

- Let them string the paper plums on the yarn to make a necklace.

- Some plastic straws can also be cut into small pieces to string between the plums to keep them separated.

Concepts: plums are oval and purple.

Skills: stringing.

Pattern 23

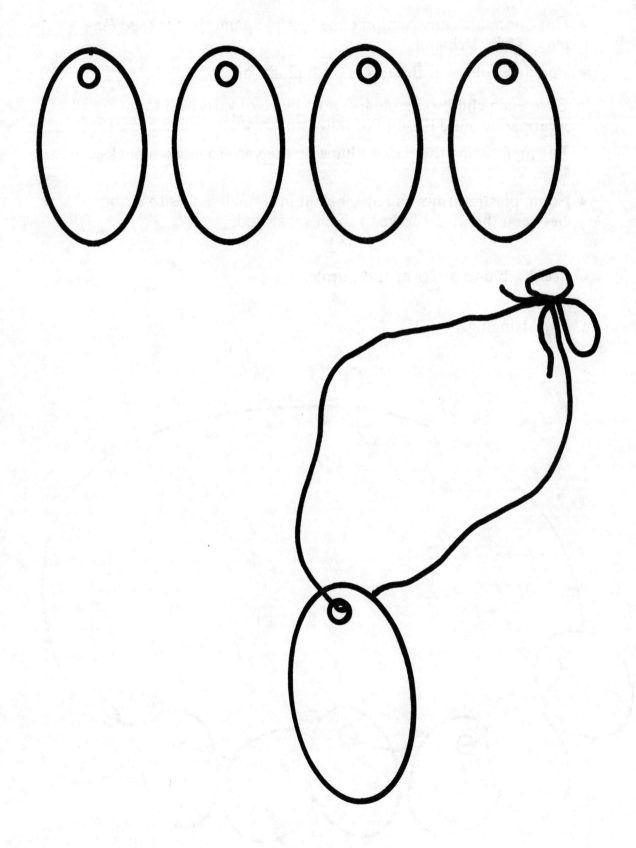

8. LANGUAGE
Real Thumb Plums

- For this activity, a large poster board activity chart *(See Pattern 24 - 6 steps)*, will need to be made in advance.

- This chart will help tell the children how to proceed with the activity of making thumb plums from baking clay.

- Place the activity chart in a highly visible location so the children can refer to it during the activity.

- Help with interpretation of the chart should always be available. *(Illustration 11)*

- Have the children make baking clay by mixing 4 cups unsifted flour, 1 1/2 cups water, and 1 cup salt together with their fingers in a bowl.

- Let the children form plums with the clay, over their thumbs.

- Bake the clay plums for about an hour at 300 degrees.

- After they have cooled, encourage the children to paint their plums purple.

Concepts: charts can explain what to do, ingredients feel different before they're mixed, baking hardens the clay.

Skills: reading a chart for directions, language development, measuring, mixing, shaping, painting.

Illustration 11

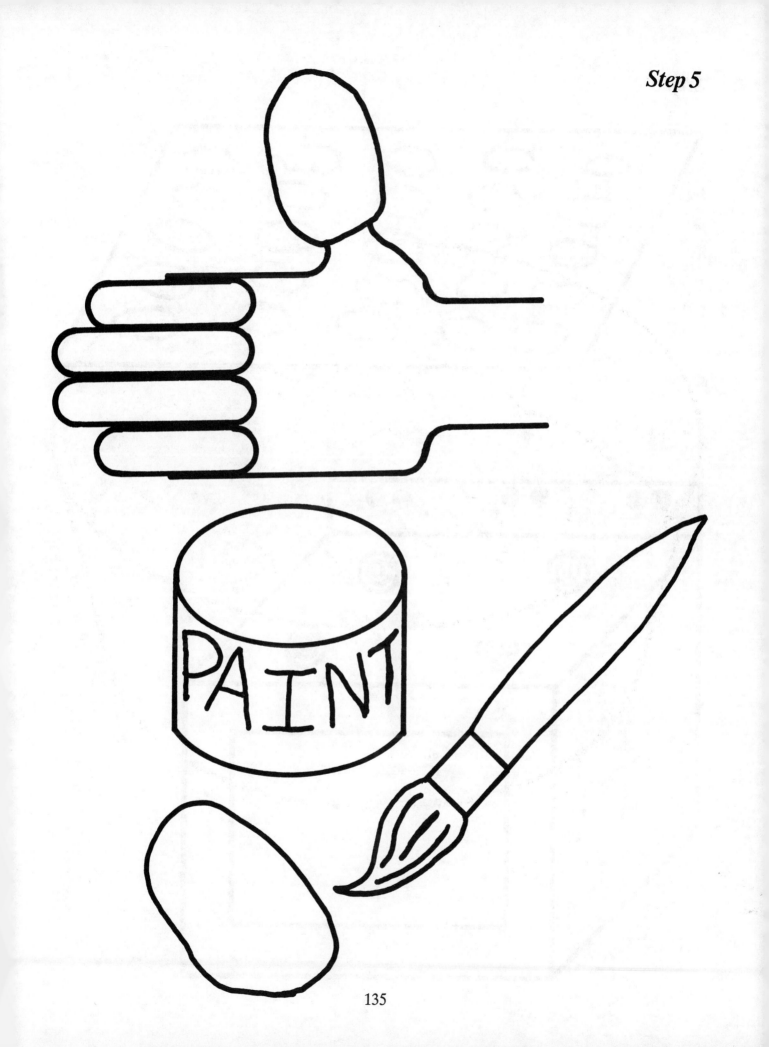

Step 6

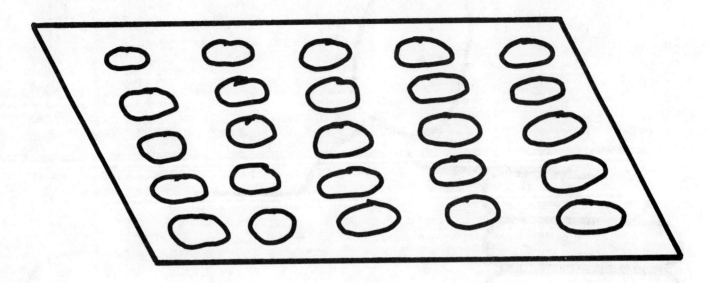

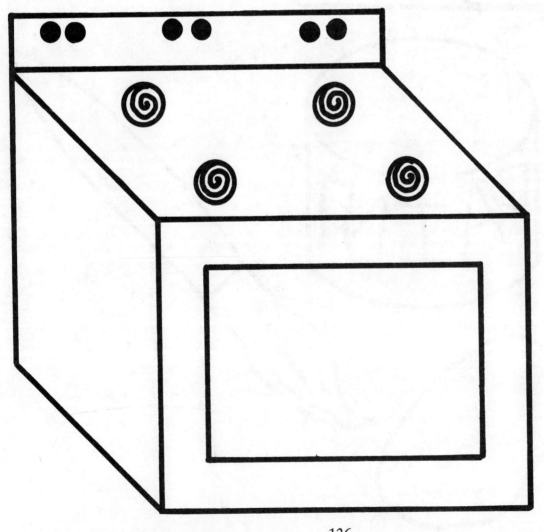